M000291193

SCOTTISH
ISLAND
BAGGING

SCOTTISH ISLAND BAGGING

THE WALKHIGHLANDS GUIDE
TO THE ISLANDS OF SCOTLAND

HELEN & PAUL WEBSTER

Vertebrate Publishing, Sheffield
www.v-publishing.co.uk

SCOTTISH ISLAND BAGGING

THE WALKHIGHLANDS GUIDE TO THE ISLANDS OF SCOTLAND

First published in 2019 by Vertebrate Publishing. Reprinted in 2019 and 2020.

VERTEBRATE PUBLISHING
Omega Court, 352 Cemetery Road, Sheffield S11 8FT, United Kingdom.
www.v-publishing.co.uk

Copyright © 2019 Helen and Paul Webster and Vertebrate Publishing Ltd.

Helen and Paul Webster have asserted their rights under the Copyright, Designs and Patents Act 1988 to be identified as authors of this work.

A CIP catalogue record for this book is available from the British Library.

ISBN 978-1-912560-30-1 (Paperback)
ISBN 978-1-912560-31-8 (Ebook)

All rights reserved. No part of this work covered by the copyright herein may be reproduced or used in any form or by any means – graphic, electronic, or mechanised, including photocopying, recording, taping, or information storage and retrieval systems – without the written permission of the publisher.

Front cover: Ben Tianavaig (Isle of Skye).
Back cover: L–R: Ring of Brodgar (Mainland Orkney), Puffin (Lunga); Goatfell (Arran), Hallival (Rum); Sands of Breckon (Yell), Up Helly Aa (Mainland Shetland); Otter, CalMac Ferry arriving at Arran. Photography by Paul and Helen Webster except where otherwise credited.

Maps produced by Don Williams of Bute Cartographics.
Contains Ordnance Survey data © Crown copyright and database right 2019.

Design and production by Jane Beagley, Vertebrate Publishing.

Printed and bound in Europe by Latitude Press.

Vertebrate Publishing is committed to printing on paper from sustainable sources.

Every effort has been made to achieve accuracy of the information in this guidebook. The authors, publishers and copyright owners can take no responsibility for: loss or injury (including fatal) to persons; loss or damage to property or equipment; trespass, irresponsible behaviour or any other mishap that may be suffered as a result of following the advice offered in this guidebook.

Opposite Shetland Mainland, Cliffs at Fethaland

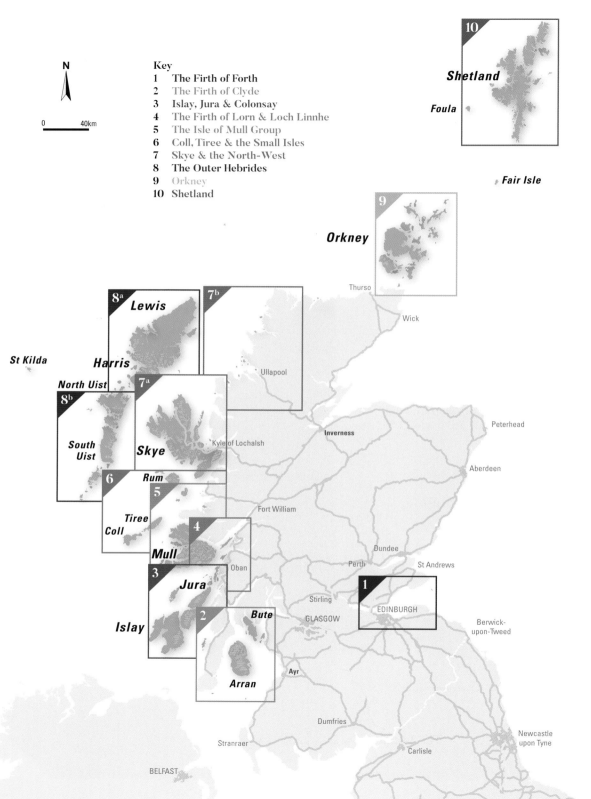

N

0   40km

Key
1   **The Firth of Forth**
2   The Firth of Clyde
3   **Islay, Jura & Colonsay**
4   **The Firth of Lorn & Loch Linnhe**
5   The Isle of Mull Group
6   **Coll, Tiree & the Small Isles**
7   **Skye & the North-West**
8   **The Outer Hebrides**
9   Orkney
10 Shetland

10 *Shetland*

Foula

Fair Isle

9 *Orkney*

Thurso

Wick

Ullapool

8a *Lewis*

Harris

7b

St Kilda

North Uist

8b

South Uist

7a

Skye

Inverness

Peterhead

Kyle of Lochalsh

Aberdeen

6 *Rum*

5

Tiree
Coll

Fort William

4

Mull

Oban

Dundee

Perth

St Andrews

3 *Jura*

2

Bute

Islay

Stirling

1

GLASGOW

EDINBURGH

Berwick-upon-Tweed

Ayr

Arran

Dumfries

Newcastle upon Tyne

Stranraer

Carlisle

BELFAST

Opposite Isle of Rum, seen from Eigg

Introduction

There's an indefinable magic about islands. Even otherwise ordinary places are transformed by a feeling of otherness when you have to cross the sea to reach them. Islands are places apart, away from the commonplace, places where we leave our normal lives behind. Just think of the words we commonly associate with them: island *escape*, island *adventure*, *treasure* island, island *paradise*.

And nowhere is this truer than with the islands of Scotland. They possess some of the finest mountain and maritime landscapes in Europe. The variety in such a compact area is immense, from the fertile fields of Orkney to the barren peatlands of Lewis, from the sandy beaches of Tiree to the Cuillin of Skye, the most alpine mountains in Britain. There are endless layers of human history to uncover too: the remarkably preserved Stone Age settlements of Skara Brae or Jarlshof, the long era of Norse rule, the richness of Gaelic culture, the human tragedy of the Clearances. Then there's the natural history: dolphins, whales, otters and some of the most spectacular seabird colonies to be found anywhere in the world.

Many people start with a visit to one of the better-known islands – Skye, Arran, or perhaps Mull; all make for experiences to remember. Once you've been to one island, the mind begins to wonder what the neighbouring islands are like – and what about the ones beyond them? All are different. If you enjoy taking trips, exploring and discovering different islands for yourself – and who wouldn't? – then you're an island bagger.

Island bagging is as addictive as Munro bagging, but it's far less precisely defined. There is no official list of islands, nor are there any rules as to what it means to bag one – so where does this book fit in?

What is an island?

The dictionary definition of an island is 'a piece of land surrounded by water'. That sounds very simple – too simple. What if it's surrounded by water only when the tide is out? What if there's a bridge? How large does it needed to be? Does a skerry or a sea stack count?

In his lavish book on Scotland's islands, beautifully illustrated with his own paintings, Hamish Haswell-Smith defines an island as:

> a piece of land or group of pieces of land which is entirely surrounded by seawater at Lowest Astronomical Tide and to which there is no permanent means of dry access.

He then further restricts himself to islands of forty hectares of more. Hamish is a yachtsman, with a passion for exploration by sea, and his book is a classic guide for those with their own boat.

Most of us, though, don't own a yacht – or even a sea kayak. We therefore focus on the islands to which it is possible to catch a ferry – or at least realistically book on to a boat trip – to make a visit. We still regard Skye and Seil as islands, despite their having bridges. We regard walking over the sands to visit a tidal island as being an unmissable adventure in itself. We're landlubbers by nature, but ones who feel the irresistible draw of the isles. We want to experience the islands in all the best ways we can.

If this sounds like you, then this is your book. Rather than restricting ourselves to strict definitions, we've focused on the ninety-nine islands that have regular trips or means of access for visitors, and have described our picks of the best ways to experience each of them. This book also features fifty-five other islands which have no regular transport but are still of significant size or interest.

How do you 'bag' an island?

Even if you are happy with whether something is an island, the question remains: what does it take to 'bag' it? Most people would say you have to at least visit it, but if you simply tag the island and leave, have you really experienced it? In 2007, Andy Strangeway announced he had 'bagged' all Scotland's islands by sleeping on them overnight.

What makes each island special? There is no one answer, and so we reckon there is no one correct way to bag an island. You might just visit it or stay overnight; you could climb its highest hill or circumnavigate its coastline. You could uncover its history, sample the local island produce or take part in a community event. Which island experience you choose is entirely up to you.

Practical matters

Every island we have included features a brief introduction, and information on how to access it if it can be done without your own boat. We then describe our choices of experiences to get the most from a visit to that island.

Note that most of Scotland's islands are relatively remote and undeveloped places. There are few formal footpaths, and the walks described include only brief details – most cross rugged terrain, a long way from help. Only a few islands have mountain rescue teams. Always ensure you carry an Ordnance Survey map and a compass, and that the walk you are attempting is within your experience and abilities. If you are heading to a tidal island make sure you have studied the tide times and allow plenty of time to return safely. If you are unsure of what you are doing or where you are going, consider hiring a guide.

1 Colonsay, Carnan Eoin   **2 Mull,** white-tailed eagle   **3 Mainland Shetland,** Up Helly Aa   **4 Mainland Orkney,** Ring of Brodgar
5 Arran, Goatfell   **6 Skye,** from the Raasay ferry terminal   **7 Islay,** Carraig Fhada

The islands featured that do not have regular boat services are for information only; these may be accessible by your own boat or kayak but this is outside the scope of this book – the waters around Scotland's islands are amongst the most challenging in the world.

A word of warning
After climbing their first few Munros, many hillwalkers find Munro bagging addictive, even if they try to resist. As they advance it can become all-consuming, taking up all their free time and dominating their thoughts. But at least Munro bagging has an end point, when that final summit is reached.

Island bagging, on the other hand, may be more dangerous. You may get a passion for it. You might even visit and experience something on every single one of the main ninety-nine islands with ferries, bridges, tidal causeways and boats as featured in this book. You might get a kayak or charter a boat to visit the other islands listed. You may work your way through all the islands listed by Haswell-Smith, or other longer lists. But whatever you do, there will always be more islands to visit, more skerries, islets, rocks and stacks to discover. You might eventually find yourself trying to land and climb one of St Kilda's towering sea stacks, or something even harder.

Once you've started, there is no cure for Scottish island bagging. You have been warned.

Bag your islands on Walkhighlands
Sign up as a registered user on Walkhighlands and log which islands you've visited. Head to *www.walkhighlands.co.uk* to get started.

Key
- Activity
- Beach
- Food and drink
- History and culture
- Nature and natural features
- Walk

Compared to the archipelagos of the west and north, Scotland's east coast has remarkably few islands. What these isles lack in size, they make up for in variety and interest. Their strategic position scattered across the Firth that divides Edinburgh from Fife, busy with ships, has ensured a rich history, and several of the islands are covered with old military fortifications. Perhaps more surprising is that they also boast two of Scotland's most spectacular colonies of seabirds.

THE FIRTH OF FORTH

Opposite Isle of May, seabird cliffs   **Overleaf** Cramond, Causeway

Crail

N

0   5km

Isle of May

F i r t h   o f   F o r t h

Glenrothes

Leven
Methil
Buckhaven

Cowdenbeath

Kirkcaldy

Fidra   Craigleith   Bass Rock

Dunfermline

North
Berwick

Inverkeithing   Inchcolm   Inchkeith

Queensferry   Cramond Island   Dunbar

Edinburgh   Musselburgh   Haddington

1

2

3

4

Isle of May

Some eight kilometres off the coast of Fife, the Isle of May guards the outermost reaches of the Firth of Forth. This emerald-green gem, defended by impressive cliffs, has long exerted a powerful draw on visitors; it was an important centre for pilgrimage in the Middle Ages, while today it is a National Nature Reserve, renowned for both its seabirds and importance as a pupping ground for grey seals.

There are regular boat trips to the island from April to September each year: the 100-seater *May Princess* and the twelve-seater fast RIB *Osprey* both operate out of Anstruther in Fife and give two to three hours ashore, while there is also a fast boat which runs from the Scottish Seabird Centre at North Berwick, over twenty kilometres away in East Lothian. There's a visitor centre on the island which is open during the season, and this gives information and offers shelter and toilets, but there are no other facilities.

Join the puffarazzi

While the May is home to breeding guillemots, razorbills, shags, cormorants, eiders and terns, and is an important station for migrants, for most people, there's one particular bird species that they really come to see – puffins. These incomparably charming and comical birds begin gathering in the sea around the island in April, and gradually move ashore. Taking a break from lives otherwise spent entirely out at sea, up to 60,000 pairs of puffins come here to breed each year, laying their eggs in burrows at the top of the cliffs. In early summer the skies over the island are alive with puffins, while below visitors try to get that perfect photo of a bird carrying a beakful of sand eels back to its burrow. In mid-August the puffins return to the seas.

See the high light – and the low light

After landing on the island and being attacked by the aggressive terns, most visitors then go hunting for their perfect puffin photo. Once satisfied, it is well worth continuing to explore: a network of paths encircles the island and visitors are asked to keep to these routes; the walk along the cliff edges is very dramatic. The May was the site of Scotland's first permanently manned lighthouse, a coal-fired beacon built in 1635. It was operated privately until 1814 when the Northern Lighthouse Board commissioned Robert Stevenson to build the current High Light, an ornate tower that resembles a Gothic castle. In 1843 a second lighthouse, the Low Light, was built to provide (with its neighbour) a pair of lights to help align ships, but the building is now used for accommodation for the researchers and volunteers who monitor the island's bird and animal life.

Bass Rock

The great granite citadel of the Bass Rock is a familiar landmark off the East Lothian coast. Rising precipitously 120 metres from the sea, its bald dome is dusted white by guano and surrounded by thousands of circling birds, making it look like a maritime snow globe. The Bass was once a prison for Covenanters and Jacobites, but these days it's renowned for being the home of the world's largest colony of gannets, with an incredible 150,000 of these huge but graceful birds breeding on the rock from February to October. The lighthouse has been unmanned since it was automated in 1988.

1 Isle of May, fast RIB **2** Isle of May, puffin with sand eels **3** Isle of May, Low Light **4** Isle of May, High Light

Gawp at gannets

Regular boat trips run out to visit Bass Rock from the Scottish Seabird Centre in North Berwick, with a choice of cruising in a catamaran or a fast rigid inflatable. The trips pass around the Bass, getting as close to the rock as is safe, and provide an incredible spectacle – and smell! The combination of bird and rock has led to the Bass being dubbed one of the wonders of the wildlife world by Sir David Attenborough.

Gannets are Britain's largest seabird, with a 1.8-metre wing span and a striking streamlined shape that enables them to dive at almost 100 km/h into the sea when fishing – looking like a harpoon fired from a gun. Every available spot on the island is occupied, and as well as diving for fish, the birds can be seen fighting, bill fencing, preening, carrying in weed, and – in July – feeding their fluffy chicks.

It's also possible to take a landing trip to the Bass, which usually gives around three hours ashore, although the seas can be rough and landings can never be guaranteed. These trips give a unique chance to get up close and intimate with the gannets, though there is the risk of being hit by their vomit!

Craigleith

This small island is just over a kilometre out from North Berwick's harbour. All eyes looking seaward from the town are drawn to the drama of the Bass Rock so that Craigleith, its nearer, less spectacular neighbour, is often forgotten and overlooked. For many years Craigleith was used as a rabbit warren – the animals were introduced to the island to act as a food source.

More recently it was home to one of Scotland's largest puffin colonies, with 28,000 pairs nesting as recently as 1999. The population was decimated after an invasive plant, tree mallow, reached the island and choked their burrows. The mallow had spread from Fidra having been planted there by lighthouse keepers to use as loo roll.

Hundreds of volunteers from the Scottish Seabird Centre have since been helping to control the mallow, and the puffin numbers have started to recover. There are no landing trips but the regular boat trips out to the Bass Rock pass close to the shores of Craigleith, giving views of its puffins, eiders, guillemots, cormorants and shags.

Fidra

Lying 500 metres off the beaches at Yellowcraig is Fidra, which at ten hectares is larger than the Bass Rock or Craigleith, through it reaches only ten metres in height. Robert Louis Stevenson was a frequent visitor to Yellowcraig, and Fidra is said to have been the model for the map in *Treasure Island*. The island has a prominent lighthouse, built by Robert Louis' father Thomas and his cousin David A. Stevenson. There are also the remains of a twelfth-century chapel. Like Craigleith, Fidra's puffin population is recovering following the removal of tree mallow. The island is well seen from Yellowcraig but there are no regular boat trips.

1 Bass Rock, gannets above the foghorn   **2** Gannet   **3** Bass Rock   **4** Fidra

Inchkeith

The strategic location of Inchkeith where the Firth of Forth begins to narrow to the north of Edinburgh has ensured its rich history. In 1493 King James IV ordered a mute woman and two small children to be moved to the island in a bizarre deprivation experiment to see what language the children would grow up to speak. It was thought this might show the original language of God; unsurprisingly the children never spoke at all. Subsequently it was used as a quarantine for sufferers of syphilis ('grandgore') – a ship carrying the sufferers sailed from Leith; later it served as a refuge for those with the plague.

Inchkeith was first fortified during the sixteenth-century wars between Scotland and England; today it is littered with the extensive remains of batteries and guns from the two world wars. Troops remained here until 1957, and lighthouse keepers until 1986. The island is now abandoned. There are no regular boat trips, but charters can be arranged through Forth Sea Safaris at North Queensferry.

Inchcolm

This green and relatively fertile island's name means the 'Isle of Columba', and the great saint was reputed to have visited in person in AD 567. Nonetheless, the island was home only to a

1 Inchcolm, Abbey   **2** Inchcolm, 'Inch Gnome'   **3** Inchcolm, seagull on defences   **4** Inchcolm, from Abbey tower

solitary hermit in 1123 when King Alexander I sought shelter here and vowed to build a monastery as thanks for his safety. Following Alexander's death the next year, it fell to his brother David I to build the current abbey dedicated to Columba. It's a very popular but memorable place to visit, and two different boat companies operate regular cruises and landing trips from Hawes Pier in South Queensferry. The landing trips usually allow around ninety minutes or so on the island, though it may be possible to return on a later sailing. There is a charge to land on the island – check whether this is included in your boat trip ticket, and there's a small visitor centre (with toilets) just beyond the jetty. As the boat pulls in you may notice the tiny islet opposite is populated with

a host of garden gnomes – and a sign declaring it to be 'Inch Gnome'; the gnomes are placed there by local boaters.

Climb the abbey bell tower

Known as the 'Iona of the East', Inchcolm Abbey boasts the finest preserved group of monastic buildings standing in Scotland. With structures dating from the twelfth to fifteenth centuries, it is a great place to poke around and explore. The cloister is remarkably complete and atmospheric, there's a rare surviving medieval fresco, and a Viking hogback tomb (now in the visitor centre), but for most people the highlight is the climb up the tiny curving stone steps to reach the top of the bell tower – with grand aerial views over the whole complex.

Stand guard over the Forth

Like most of the islands in the Firth of Forth, Inchcolm is littered with defences from the two world wars. These were first manned in 1915, but reworked with much heavier armaments in 1916 and 1917, with prominent batteries and gun emplacements at both ends of the island; the island was then rearmed in 1939 and the abbey was used as a barracks for a time. The ruins at the eastern end are the most fascinating to explore – you can still pass through an access tunnel to reach parts of them, though take care as the site is decaying and overgrown in places. The views across the Firth to Inchkeith, Cramond, Edinburgh and Fife reveal what a key defensive location this was. The ruins at the western end are guarded by extremely aggressive gulls and access is restricted during part of the nesting season.

Cramond Island

Linked to beautiful Cramond village and beaches by a tidal causeway, this is very much Edinburgh's island. The crossing is on a concrete causeway, but is only possible for up to two hours each side of low tide. The tide comes in very fast and many people have become stranded on the island, so make sure you pay close attention to the times which are posted on a sign near the start of the causeway. They are also available on the Queensferry lifeboat website. Do not attempt to cross anywhere but the causeway.

Make the tidal crossing

The fact that the causeway is submerged most of the time makes a visit to Cramond feel like a real adventure. There's a steep flight of steps to descend before beginning the walk across, which is further than it looks, being well over a kilometre. The concrete pylons alongside the causeway were built to stop enemy boats during the Second World War, not submarines as often supposed, as the water isn't deep enough for the latter. From the far end of Cramond an anti-boat and submarine boom then extended on to reach the tiny islet of Inchmickery, then on to Inchcolm and finally to the Fife coast.

Once on the island a rough path heads up to the highest point, a superb viewpoint for the Forth, with the defences on neighbouring Inchmickery covering it so completely that it looks like a battleship. You can continue from here to pass the ruins of an old farm and the various old gun emplacements, but make sure you leave plenty of time to get back across the causeway before the rising tide.

1 Cramond Island, defences   **2** Inchmickery

The halcyon days of the paddle steamers carrying thousands of workers from Glasgow 'down the watter' to holiday on these isles may be long gone, but Arran, Bute and Great Cumbrae remain popular destinations with folk from Scotland's biggest city and beyond. The largest island, Arran, boasts not just one of Scotland's most dramatic mountain ranges, but lowlands and rich history too, while Rothesay on Bute and Millport on Cumbrae retain the charm of seaside resorts from years gone by. Beyond these, there are real gems amongst the smaller isles of the Firth, from the cliffs and gannetries of Ailsa Craig to the remarkable cave painting on the tidal island of Davaar.

THE FIRTH OF CLYDE

Opposite Bute, West Island Way   **Overleaf** Arran coast path, near Hutton's Unconformity

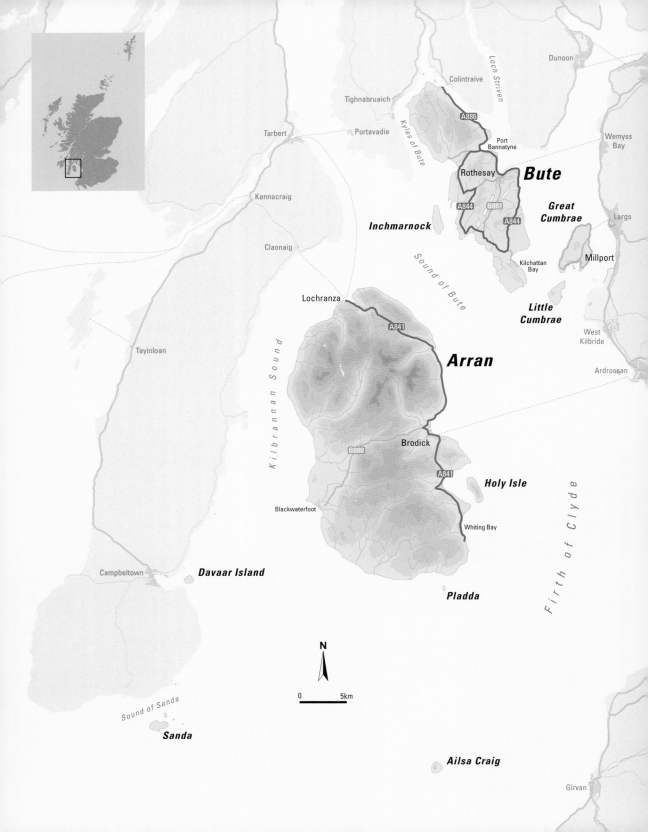

Arran

Often described as Scotland in miniature, Arran offers a remarkable variety of activities and scenery in a relatively compact island package. From atmospheric prehistoric stone circles, to challenging mountain walks which rank amongst the most spectacular in the Scottish hills, all encircled by a fine coast of sandy beaches, caves and high cliffs. Not to mention the cultural sights, wildlife, whisky and quality local produce from this unique island that is home to around 4,000 people.

Arran is very accessible from Glasgow, making it a popular weekend destination year round. Caledonian MacBrayne (CalMac) vehicle ferries run from Ardrossan (with a train connection to Glasgow), taking around an hour to reach Brodick – it's best to book if you are taking your car. There is also a shorter ferry route from Claonaig (in Kintyre) to Lochranza which operates in the summer months, and a longer daily service from Tarbert to Lochranza in the winter. Arran has a great bus service which makes public transport a feasible option if you're prepared to do a bit of planning and be flexible. The main services and shops are in Brodick; there is a range of accommodation here and scattered across the island.

Climb Goatfell

The highest mountain on Arran at 874 metres, Goatfell is also one of the easier peaks to climb amongst Arran's granite mountain ridges. The ascent can be rewarded with superb views all around, even reaching Ireland on the clearest of days. The most straightforward ascent is from near Brodick; the out-and-back route from there can be completed in a long half day if you are fit. If you want to really push it, the Goatfell Race takes place each year in May – the fastest runners complete the course in under an hour

and a quarter! There are a number of other ways up, including ones taking in some of the other dramatic peaks seen from the summit, many of which require some scrambling. While you'd be lucky to spot any wild goats here (the Goat part of the name either comes from the Gaelic word *gaoth*, meaning wind, or from the Norse word for goat, *geita*), keep an eye out for golden eagles and buzzards riding the thermals.

Bike around the island

The full circumnavigation of the island on two wheels is a popular goal for cyclists. Most tackle this tough eighty-eight-kilometre road route clockwise to get the big hills out of the way early, and to take advantage of the downhill last few kilometres to freewheel back to the ferry. The fittest cyclists can complete the circuit in four hours, but with plenty of pretty villages and inviting refuelling spots along the way, many take a whole day – keep those legs moving to ensure you don't miss the last ferry. Bikes are carried free on CalMac ferries and there is also bike hire available in Brodick.

Feel the ancient past at Machrie Moor

A walk of a kilometre from a car park leads you into this intriguing prehistoric site. Six stone circles can be made out in total, including one with huge sandstone blocks up to five and a half metres high. Others are constructed from smaller granite rocks, and there are also remains of burial chambers, hut circles and ancient field systems to discover. It is thought that the site was used for ceremonial purposes 4,500 years ago, with the visible stone circles dating back to 2000 BC. As they stand in open moorland and require the short walk, you can often be alone amongst the stones, adding to the atmosphere.

Walk the Arran coast

Fitting neatly into a week, the complete Arran Coastal Way is a long-distance walk around the island with a couple of optional inland excursions. Don't be fooled by the low level of this walk, there are some very rugged sections of coastline to negotiate – as well as the optional ascent of Goatfell. With careful planning the route can be completed using a mix of B&Bs, hotels and hostels, or from a central base using the bus service, as well as by backpacking and enjoying some stunning wild camping spots.

If you don't have time for the complete circuit, the most spectacular section of the Coastal Way can be walked as a fine day route. It clings to the coast between Sannox and Lochranza, passing the Cock of Arran, a giant boulder resembling a cockerel.
www.walkhighlands.co.uk/arran/arran-coastal-way.shtml

Hear the rut at Lochranza

The village of Lochranza on the north-west coast is home to a herd of red deer that seem immune to the disturbance of people, happily munching away or obligingly posing in front of the castle while their photos are taken. In fact, they can pose a hazard on the golf course, oblivious to shouts of 'fore'. They are not tame and should not be approached or fed; their wildness becomes more apparent during the autumnal rut when it can be enchanting or terrifying – perhaps both – to hear the stags roaring, depending on whether you are hearing this from the comfort of a B&B or cowering in a tent at Lochranza's campsite.

Find Hutton's Unconformity

The geologist James Hutton came to Arran in 1787 and made a remarkable discovery. Near Newton Point on the coast between Sannox and Lochranza he found older rocks sitting on top of younger ones. This became known as Hutton's Unconformity; he went on to find other similar examples and began to develop his revolutionary thinking about the processes of geology. Newton Point is easily reached on foot by heading along the road on the east side of Loch Ranza and continuing on the path to the headland. Extend the walk into a five-kilometre circuit by following the coast to the cottage at Fairy Dell and returning on an inland path and track.

Watch for a spider at King's Cave

The King's Cave is a dramatic sea cave – now above high tide level – on the west coast of the island. It was here that Robert the Bruce is said to have had his famed encounter with the spider following a series of defeats, and from it he gained his resolve to 'try, try again' – ultimately winning Scottish independence at the Battle of Bannockburn. Several other Scottish caves also claim to be the site of this legend, but the King's Cave is the finest of them. Enjoy the fine coastal setting on the approach, taking a torch to enable you to seek out the ancient carvings inside including ones of a cross, horse and deer. The four-and-a-half-kilometre circular route is best tackled from the Torr Righ Beag forestry car park north of Blackwaterfoot.

1 Arran, north ridge of Goatfell **2** Red deer **3** Arran, Machrie Moor **4** Arran, cheese
5 Arran, ferry and Goatfell **6** Arran, King's Cave

Visit the Glenashdale Falls

This spectacular waterfall is one of Arran's showplaces and makes a fine highlight of a walk from Whiting Bay. The viewing platform near the top of the falls is the best place to admire the two graceful tiers of the cascade. Start from the parking area at the southern end of Whiting Bay and follow the signed path up through enchanting old woodland. The Giant's Graves (actually two chambered cairns) can be visited on the same route – to continue to them, keep climbing and turn left at a track, following this for another kilometre until a signed path off to the cairns and their stunning viewpoint; the path then returns to the village.

See the seals at Kildonan

Walk along the sandy shore at Kildonan at low tide and you're pretty much guaranteed to encounter some of Arran's large colony of common seals. Hauled out on the rocks, they often flip themselves into banana shapes with their head and tails aloft as if performing some core-strengthening exercise at the gym. Youngsters can be spotted from late summer onwards. Take great care not to cause a disturbance by getting too close. The rest of the shoreline here is a great place for rock-pooling and looking for otters.

Visit Brodick Castle

An imposing Scots Baronial pile, Brodick Castle stands on the site of a much earlier fortress from the fifth century. The current elegant country house is today owned by the National Trust for Scotland and is said to be haunted by no less than three ghosts, including a grey lady who apparently perished in the castle's dungeon having been left to starve there as she was suffering from the plague. You can explore the surrounding country park and its trails for free – be sure to seek out the twelve-sided Bavarian summer house beautifully lined with pine cones. *www.nts.org.uk/visit/places/brodick-castle-garden-country-park*

Pass the twelve apostles at Catacol

When much of Arran was turned over to deer and became a sporting estate, a high number of local people were cleared from the interior of the island. This attractive row of houses at Catacol was built as part of an attempt to encourage the farmers to look to fishing for a new livelihood. Each top-floor window is a different shape, the idea being that a wife could summon her husband back from the sea by lighting a candle in the window of their own house. The reality is that most people who had been evicted from their original houses left the island, but this row of cottages remains as a memorial to a time of change.

Taste a dram at Lochranza

Arran distillery opened in 1995, ending a dry period in whisky production for the island as the last legal distillery closed in 1837. The new distillery sits in Lochranza and is one of only a few independent distillers in Scotland. A range of tours is available, from a basic introduction to the art of distilling to tutored tastings with a stillman. There is also a cafe on site. For a total immersion you could do worse than spend a summer weekend at the annual Malt and Music festival which includes the chance to select the festival bottling for the following year. *www.arranwhisky.com*

1 Arran, Twelve Apostles **2** Arran, Brodick Castle **3** Arran, Glenashdale Falls **4** Arran, Kildonan seals

Sample Arran cheese and oatcakes

Head to the Isle of Arran Cheese Shop near Brodick and nibble on tasty samples of the wax-wrapped flavoured cheddars. You can watch the cheese being made through a viewing window. Head to Blackwaterfoot to try award-winning cheeses from the Bellevue Creamery, including Arran Blue, Arran Camembert and an Arran Crowdie (a cream cheese often rolled in oats). Continue your cheese tour in the south of the island at Torrylinn Creamery where you can also watch the cheesemakers at work as well as sampling their wares including delicious ice cream. Of course no cheese would be complete in Scotland without an oatcake – head to Wooleys bakery in Brodick which has been producing its signature oatcakes since the mid-nineteenth century.

Try the ArranMan Triathlon

Held in September when the sea may just have warmed up a tad, this fitness fest includes an open-water swim from Holy Isle to Lamlash and a half Ironman, as well as Olympic and sprint triathlon distances. An evening ceilidh brings events to a finish in the unlikely event you have any excess energy to use up.

Arran's music festivals

Arran's long-running folk festival, held in June, has now been joined by a two-day festival which combines whisky and music and is held towards the end of the month at Lochranza distillery. Both feature a survivors' party on the Sunday after the main celebrations.

Pladda

This tiny, tear-shaped and low-lying island is less than a kilometre long. It boasts a lighthouse and was once home to the keepers and their families. Supplies would be ferried by boat four times a month with some visits timed so that the lighthouse keepers could attend church. In later years helicopters took over the supply role, and eventually the lighthouse was automated in 1990 and is now monitored remotely from Edinburgh. The island is uninhabited.

Holy Isle

Holy Isle consists of a single dramatic hill falling steeply on all sides to the sea, situated in Lamlash Bay. The island is owned by the Kagyu Samye Ling Buddhist community which uses it for spiritual retreats.

A ferry runs from April to October with other sailings on request; it's always best to check there will be space and that the ferry will be running before you plan to go. Day visitors to the island are usually met by a volunteer for a quick chat about the isle, the conservation projects and the community. Longer stays are possible as part of a Buddhist retreat or by working as a volunteer.

www.holyisle.org

Climb to the top of Mullach Mòr

Take the short ferry ride from Lamlash and climb to the highest point on Holy Isle to experience a very different view of Arran. The fluttering Tibetan flags that greet visitors are a reminder that the island is run by a Buddhist community. The climb to the highest point is rough and steep but reasonably straightforward, following

---

1 Pladda, from Arran, with distant Ailsa Craig   **2 Holy Isle,** from Lamlash

a path up through native woodland and on to open heather moorland before a final ridge and the true top at 314 metres. Keep an eye out for the Eriskay ponies, Saanen goats and Soay sheep who call the island home. You can complete a seven-kilometre circuit by descending to the Centre for World Peace and Health at the south end of the island and returning along the coast, discovering the brightly painted thangka artworks along the shore. Religious retreat and contemplation is nothing new here – St Molaise spent twenty years living as a hermit in a cave in the sixth century. Today a day visit more than satisfies most island baggers.

Bute

The Isle of Bute is undergoing something of a revival as visitors once again come to cherish the Victorian elegance of the main settlement Rothesay and the charming scenery of this green and fertile island. Long established as a day trip destination for Glasgow folk who packed steamers on the Clyde in the first half of the nineteenth century, and a holiday home favourite for rich industrialists who built fancy villas on the seafront, it retains an olde worlde charm, giving the illusion of remoteness while actually being within easy reach. With a population of just over 6,000 it manages to retain that friendly island feel.

The main ferry to Bute sails from Wemyss Bay and connects with the train from Glasgow. It takes thirty-five minutes and docks at Rothesay and runs about every hour. There is also a ferry from Colintraive on the Cowal peninsula that reaches the north end of the island at Rhubodach; this crossing takes only five minutes and also runs half-hourly. Both ferries carry vehicles and passengers.

Spend a penny at the Victorian toilets

Surely ranking amongst the most ornate of public toilets, these date from 1899 during Rothesay's heyday as a Victorian resort. Located just beyond the ferry pier, every inch is clad in tiles or mosaic to give an opulent first impression to visitors – male visitors, that is; Victorian women were not catered for and the adjoining modern ladies' toilets are quite a contrast. The attendant will usually let females have a peek in the mens' when they are empty. Needless to say, it costs more than a penny these days.

Go Gothic at Mount Stuart

Prepare for a sensory feast at this Gothic Revival extravaganza of a mansion built in the late 1870s. The house is the ancestral home of the Stuarts of Bute, scions of Robert the Bruce by virtue of being descended from the illegitimate son of King Robert II of Scotland. The current house replaces one which burnt down, and is an incredible feast of ornate carving, marble colonnades, a star-studded ceiling, a huge tapestry, and spires and turrets carved from red stone.

It's worth taking your time and seeking out the animals hiding amongst the carved foliage on the decorated wood panelling which adorns many of the rooms, or the doorknobs, all different and expertly crafted by hand. The house also incorporates the trappings of modernity and is said to have been the first house to have an indoor heated swimming pool (though the Romans may have something to say on this one) and the first Scottish home to boast electric lighting in addition to a lift and a telephone system. The extensive grounds are well worth exploring, with formal gardens giving way to landscaped parkland with a variety of walks.
www.mountstuart.com

1 Bute, Mount Stuart interior 2 Bute, Rothesay Victorian toilets 3 Bute, Mount Stuart

Hike the West Island Way

You've heard of its big brother, now escape the crowds and tackle this forty-five-kilometre long-distance walking route. It can be walked as an epic one-day challenge, or more leisurely two- or three-day options. The bus service allows you to stop and start at various points. Traditionally starting with a southern loop around Kilchattan Bay, it then crosses the centre of the island before looping again at the north end, taking in scenic coastline, fertile pastures and rugged moors.
www.walkhighlands.co.uk/argyll/west-island-way.shtml

Wave at a boat from Canada Hill

Climb to this viewpoint above Rothesay where families of emigrating Bute folk would gather to catch a final glimpse of the ships carrying their relatives away and on towards the New World. Many headed to Nova Scotia in Canada in the mid to late 1800s. Today there is a Rothesay in the Canadian province of New Brunswick and many Canadians can trace their heritage back to Bute. The walk from Rothesay takes in the thirteen mini-hairpins of Serpentine Hill which at an average ten per cent gradient is a challenge for cyclists, even boasting its own annual hill race, often completed in under two minutes. If on foot, there are steps alongside and the rest of the walk is much less strenuous, heading through farmland to reach the trig point and bench that marks the summit of Canada Hill.

1 Bute, below Canada Hill   **2 Bute**, Rothesay from Serpentine en route to Canada Hill
3 Bute, St Blane's Church   **4 Bute**, Ettrick Bay

See St Blane's Church

These extensive and atmospheric ruins are visited on the first circular stage of the West Island Way or by a short ramble from the road. Most of the remains that you can see date back to AD 1100, but the site was a very early Christian monastery established by St Catan back as far as AD 500. St Blane was his nephew and began his spiritual life here and at Kingarth. In addition to the church ruins, remnants of the community that once served the religious buildings also survive, including a well and the remains of a manse.

Relax at Ettrick Bay

A mile-long expanse of sand makes Ettrick Bay the most popular beach on Bute, but it never feels crowded. Grab an ice cream from the shoreside tearoom and ramble across the sands. In contrast to the peaceful scene today, the sands were used as one of a number of training grounds for the D-Day landings during the Second World War. For a wilder-feeling beach, head to Stravanan Bay in the south of the island. It lies on the West Island Way and it is possible to visit it as part of a circular walk from Kilchattan Bay, also visiting a prehistoric stone circle.

Go to ButeFest

Held at the end of July and billed as 'more than just a music festival', ButeFest aims to bring music, art and cultural experiences to islanders and visitors alike. The family-friendly event takes place in the stunning scenery of Ettrick Bay, meaning anyone can slope off for a bit of sand and surf at any time.

Inchmarnock

Lying just to the west of and easily visible from Bute, Inchmarnock has a long history of habitation. It was named for St Marnock who established a monastery on the island in the seventh century. An archaeological dig unearthed a number of incised slates which experts have concluded were used for learning to read and write, much as slates were still used in schools well into the twentieth century. The finds included the Hostage Stone, a medieval 'doodle' showing a prisoner, who may be a monk, being dragged towards a boat with another figure holding a church-shaped relic; it perhaps tells of a Viking raid and helps us to understand how such valuable objects came to be found in Norse graves far away. The stone is now held by the National Museum of Scotland. More recently during the nineteenth century Inchmarnock was used as a remote naughty step for misbehaving drunks from Bute who would be abandoned on the island until they had dried out. Now turned over to farming, the population was evacuated during the Second World War so that the island could be used for commando training, including for the D-Day landings on the Normandy beaches.

Great Cumbrae

It may not look like one, but the CalMac ferry which crosses from Largs to Cumbrae is in fact a time machine. In the short time it takes to cross the water, passengers are whisked back to a sleepier age. The grandeur of the coastal villas of Millport, the palms and swing boats that adorn the prom, and the small independent cafes and shops give a gentle nostalgic feel to this holiday island. Many visitors do come for more active pursuits, with an emphasis on water sports, the sheltered waters being perfect for kayaking, sailing and stand-up paddle boarding.

The ferry from Largs (with train connections to Glasgow) takes just eight and a half minutes to cross Largs Bay. A bus meets the ferry for the short ride to the main settlement of Millport or there is a pleasant cross-country walking route.

Cycle around Cumbrae

At roughly four kilometres long by two kilometres wide, and boasting a tranquil, flattish coastal road, Cumbrae is the perfect island for a gentle bike ride. The sixteen-kilometre circuit is regularly tackled by families and there are places to stop for refreshments en route as well as coastal bays to spot birds and seals. Bike hire is available in Millport, including e-bikes, tag-alongs and even an eight-seater where everyone is facing inwards and seemingly pedalling towards each other – luckily the laid-back vibe of the island extends to local drivers who are used to slow or erratic cyclists.

Discover Cumbrae's wedgie and wee cathedral

Cumbrae does quirky, boasting the world's narrowest house – find The Wedge squeezed in between a couple of shops on Millport's

1 Great Cumbrae, Cathedral of the Isles **2** Great Cumbrae, with Arran behind

seafront. A mere 120 centimetres wide at the front, the property opens out towards the back but is still only 335 centimetres at its widest point. If you like things diminutive, the island also boasts Britain's smallest cathedral. Situated in a beautiful wooded glade, the Gothic-style Cathedral of the Isles can be reached by following Cow Lane at the rear of Millport.

Power yourself to the island summit

While it is possible to drive almost to the highest point on the island, the walk or bike up to the trig point at a mere 127 metres above sea level is easy enough and the reward of fabulous views in all directions is that much more satisfying. Topped by a red sandstone boulder known as the Glaid Stone and bearing the names of many previous visitors, there is

also a trig point nearby. The handy viewpoint helps you identify landmarks on neighbouring Arran and the mainland.

Enjoy an ice cream at the crocodile rock

For well over a century visiting children and those just young at heart have enjoyed climbing on the back of the crocodile which lounges on the west side of Millport's seafront. It is thought the rock was originally painted by local man Robert Brown in 1913 – possibly after he'd had a lunchtime pint or two. The rock itself is probably well over 4.5 million years old, but its crocodile grin, washed by the tide twice a day, makes it a firm favourite with visitors. Best enjoyed with an ice cream – check out the locally made ones from the Ritz Cafe or the Isle of Cumbrae Ice Cream shop.

1 Great Cumbrae, crocodile rock   **2** Little Cumbrae   **3** Great Cumbrae, summit   **4** Ailsa Craig, from Girvan

Little Cumbrae

Known locally as Wee Cumbrae, this small rocky island lies less than a kilometre from its larger sibling and boasts a lighthouse, farm and palatial early twentieth-century mansion with gardens designed by Gertrude Jekyll. The island is privately owned and yoga retreats are run from the house. Little Cumbrae even has its own tiny island sibling – Castle Island, complete with impressive tower castle, is only accessible at low tide.

Ailsa Craig

The volcanic plug of Ailsa Craig rises dramatically from the sea some fourteen kilometres out from the Ayrshire coast. Its position halfway between Belfast and Glasgow has earned it the nickname 'Paddy's Milestone', and its domed summit is certainly an impressive viewpoint. Now a bird reserve, the island's smooth granite is the source of well over half the world's curling stones. There are many other signs of man here, from early habitation in the caves on the island, the remains of a sixteenth-century castle built to deter Spaniards from grabbing the strategic island, and more recently a lighthouse with four keepers' cottages which

were occupied until the light was automated in 1990.

Day passenger trips to Ailsa Craig run daily from Girvan in the summer months. Landing, and the amount of time you'll get on the island, is dependent on the sea conditions and tides. The trips are increasingly popular so it is advisable to book, bearing in mind that weather-prone cancellations are common.

Climb the Craig

The very steep and strenuous climb to the summit is rewarded with breathtaking views and a head-spinning sensation of being in the air as it's impossible to see the coastline of Ailsa Craig from its currant-bun-like summit.

Reaching the top is a challenge which shouldn't be underestimated, and not all boat trips allow enough time to make the ascent. It's best to go early in the season before the bracken completely impedes the lower half of the route, although the swathes of bluebells can also be slippery underfoot. A path starts near a square bothy at the base of the cliffs and takes a diagonal line to reach a broad shelf and the ruins of the castle. From here the gradient steepens and only a trace of a path continues heading uphill, eventually petering out before the trig point marking the highest point is reached. On a clear day Ireland can clearly be seen as well as Arran, Kintyre and Ayrshire.

Cruise around the Craig's backside

The impressive gannetries and other seabird colonies are mainly on the high cliffs on the far side of the Craig, and simply must be seen. A few puffins also now nest here following the eradication of rats in 1991. In decent weather most of the boat trips will take an exploratory detour on the return trip to view the cliffs and circumnavigate the island. The water is also the best place to view the massive foghorns, one in the south and one in the north of the island. Built in 1866 and initially powered by compressed air, they warned ships of the notorious shipwreck spot for a hundred years. From the boat you can also see the almost inaccessible Swine Cave, supposedly where original inhabitants of the Craig sheltered their pigs during bad weather; it is also said to have been used by smugglers.

Davaar Island

Davaar Island is linked by a natural tidal causeway to the Kintyre peninsula, near Campbeltown. Its strategic position led to a lighthouse being built (a Stevenson family effort of course) in 1854; a lookout building was added nearby to overlook the anti-submarine nets that protected Campbeltown during the Second World War. Walking to Davaar is an adventure in itself,

1 Ailsa Craig, summit   **2** Ailsa Craig, cruise around the cliffs
3 Davaar Island, crucifixion cave   **4** Ailsa Craig, the castle   **5** Davaar Island

as the shingle causeway known as An Doirlinn is only exposed for around three hours either side of low tide. Check tide times and aim to start your crossing just as the waters part to allow sufficient time to explore Davaar Island. Ensure you leave plenty of time for the return crossing and do not attempt to cross when the tide is coming in – the crossing is well over a kilometre long and there have been fatalities here.

Pay your respects at the crucifixion cave

Once you have done your best King Canute impressions and walked across the spectacular causeway, keep to the right to head towards the high cliffs on the south side of the island. You'll pass a number of sea caves, some of which are worth a quick explore, but the one you're aiming

for is special due to a painting discovered by fishermen in 1887 and thought at the time to be the work of God. In fact the large rendering of Jesus on the cross had been painted in secret by local school art teacher Archibald MacKinnon. The work has been repainted many times, the task usually being undertaken by the art teacher at Campbeltown school.

Sanda

This small island is well seen from Arran's southern coastline. It was home to a bird observatory, and was inhabited until very recently. The tall lighthouse which sits above two smaller towers and an arch resembles a ship when seen from the sea.

The southernmost of the Hebrides are islands of stark contrasts. The largest, Islay, is the closest of Scotland's isles to Ireland and, green and fertile, it is dubbed the 'Queen of the Hebrides'. Close neighbour Jura is as wild and rugged as anywhere in the Highlands, its interior a mix of moorland and gaunt, scree-clad peaks, with settlements clinging only to its eastern strip. The smaller Colonsay is more remote but is a complete delight, mixing idyllic beaches, a distinctive community and a landscape punctuated with miniature rocky peaks.

ISLAY, JURA & COLONSAY

Opposite Colonsay, Traigh Ban   **Overleaf** Jura, Craighouse

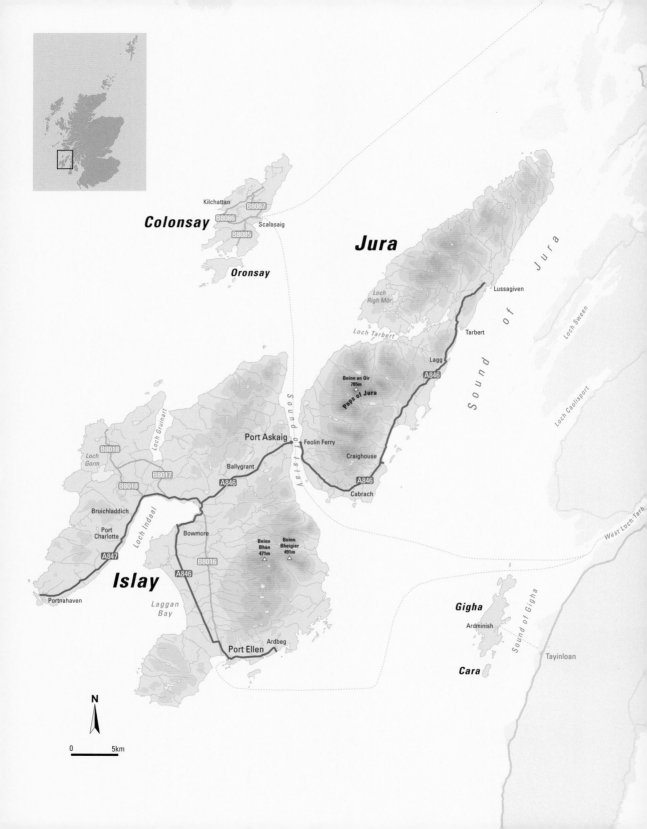

Islay

You can almost catch the smell of the angels' share on Islay's sea breezes. This island – even more than Speyside – is regarded as the spiritual home of Scotch whisky, and the names of its distilleries are famed worldwide for their rich, peaty malts. But there's much more to the island than the water of life. Islay is known as the 'Queen of the Hebrides' and is blessed with picturesque whitewashed villages, unique birdlife, fine sandy beaches and a rugged coastline worthy of exploration.

Islay is well served by large CalMac vehicle ferries from Kennacraig on the Kintyre peninsula. These sail two or three times a day, landing at either the village of Port Ellen in the south (2 hours 10 mins), or tiny Port Askaig (2 hours 5 mins) overlooking Jura, and most have connecting bus links from Glasgow. In the summer there's also a weekly ferry from Oban, via Colonsay. Islay has an airport at Glenegedale, served by three daily flights from Glasgow in the summer and two in the winter, as well as a twice-a-week day return service from Oban and Colonsay.

The island has a wide range of accommodation, shops and places to eat, and all the main villages are linked by bus.

Discover the water of life

With nine working distilleries, many in picturesque seaside locations, Islay is simply *the* place to sample a dram. Laphroaig, Lagavulin and Ardbeg distilleries on the south coast are the island's most famous and heavily peated. It's fascinating to see behind the scenes, inhale the heady brewery scent from the giant vats of bubbling wort and check out the vast quantities of whisky maturing for years in the bonded warehouses. It's also a great way to warm up on a dreich and rainy day. The distilleries offer standard tours and tastings of their main

single malts, but also more specialist tours designed to appeal to the real connoisseur. These are often in intimate small groups with the opportunity to sample some of their rarer expressions. Laphroaig, Lagavulin and Ardbeg can all be visited on foot or by bike on a dedicated six-kilometre path from Port Ellen, although it's best to book the actual tours in advance. Ardbeg – the last of the three – has a very fine cafe, and you can even return to Port Ellen by bus if you're feeling a little wobbly at the end of your adventures in malt.

Get twitching

Islay is a heaven for birdwatchers, renowned for the chance to see rare species like the chough and the corncrake, and for the many thousands of overwintering geese who migrate from the Arctic to munch on Islay's verdant grass. Head to the RSPB centre at Loch Gruinart to visit hides overlooking the loch and check the recent sightings – during the winter months a dawn or dusk visit can be spectacular as the geese arrive or depart to and from their favourite grazing spots. Spring brings masses of migrating birds including plenty of rare oddities blown off course and taking shelter on the island for a short while. The coastal cliffs support a wide variety of seabirds including nesting puffins on the Oa peninsula – also a good place to look out for golden eagles and hen harriers.

Pay your respects to the Lords of the Isles

Islay has an important place in the history of Scotland's islands, and there are a several sites in stunningly scenic locations which no visitor can afford to miss. First stop for history buffs should be Finlaggan, a few kilometres from Port Askaig. On an island on a loch here lived the Lords of the Isles who ruled a large kingdom across the west of Scotland from the thirteenth to the fifteenth centuries. Today you can walk across a boardwalk to visit the site and see the remains

of a castle and chapel, together with some very fine carved sixteenth-century gravestones and numerous archaeological artefacts.

Visit Bowmore's round church

This striking circular building dominates Bowmore from its position at the top of the Main Street. It was built in the 1760s, and its roof is supported by a massive central oak pillar and walls that are almost a metre thick.

See Kildalton Cross

This ancient carved cross in the remote graveyard of Kildalton Church is regarded as the finest surviving example of early Celtic Christian carving. Dating from AD 800, it features the classic spiral and knot work around two roundels, Christ as a lion, the Virgin and Child, and scenes including Cain killing Abel, the sacrifice of Isaac, and David slaying a lion. There's another very fine cross at Kilchoman on the Rinns peninsula.

Machir Bay and Kilchoman

Islay has some superb beaches, including Laggan Bay which stretches for over seven kilometres along the east coast. The finest, however, is Machir Bay on the Rinns peninsula – a perfect expanse of golden sand backed by dunes and just a short walk from a car park. Before leaving, be sure to visit the nearby Kilchoman distillery. Opened in only 2005, this was the first new distillery on Islay for 124 years, but its traditional methods are a contrast to the mass production of its big-name rivals. It uses barley grown on its own farm, and is one of only six distilleries in Scotland to still carry out all its own traditional floor maltings. Non-whisky buffs will enjoy the cafe which serves the finest Victoria sponge cake you can imagine.

Mull of Oa

The Oa peninsula is Islay at its most rugged, a wild moorland fringed with fine sea cliffs. Its final headland – the Mull of Oa – is the site of the dramatic American Monument, perched 130 metres above the waves. Towards the end of the First World War, a massive troop ship carrying over 2,000 US soldiers was torpedoed off the Oa. Although other boats in the convoy quickly began a rescue mission, many men drowned and in some cases lifeboats were dashed against the high cliffs. The stories of locals rescuing survivors and providing dignified burials for many of the lost are very poignant and can be explored at the fascinating Museum of Islay Life in Port Charlotte. The American Monument commemorates both this disaster and the shipwreck of the HMS *Otranto* in 1918 with the loss of over 350 souls. There's a waymarked three-kilometre circular walk out to the Mull from the car park at the end of the road.

Bag the Beinn

At 491 metres high, Beinn Bheigier doesn't rival the great Paps on neighbouring Jura, however as the highest point on Islay it does command fabulous views; the summit can usually be enjoyed in splendid solitude as the hike up involves tough, pathless terrain that deters many. The usual start point is the end of the road at Claggain Bay on the east coast. An often sodden path can be followed via Ardtalla to the empty cottage at Proaig, from where a stiff walk through deep heather leads up to the summit. If you fancy walking company, the island hosts an annual festival in April that usually takes in guided walks on Colonsay and Jura as well.

---

1 Islay, Ardbeg distillery   **2** Islay, Soldier's Rock   **3** Islay, Portnahaven   **4** Islay, on Beinn Bheigier   **5** Islay, Machir Bay
6 Islay, Kildalton Cross   **7** Islay, Bowmore round church   **8** Islay, American Monument

Fèis Île

Islay's annual 'music and malt festival' is held at the end of May and combines a varied programme of tunes, songs, history, piping, Gaelic workshops, and just the occasional dram at special distillery open days, as well as friendly ceilidhs and food-themed events. For those seeking an even more laid-back vibe there's an annual jazz festival too – held in September, it's also sponsored by a whisky producer.
www.islayfestival.com

Islay Book Festival

Held every September, the Islay Book Festival has a varied literary programme, often featuring books with a connection to the water of life, of course.
www.islaybookfestival.co.uk

Beach rugby tournament

Each June, over a thousand spectators watch thirty teams of both sexes battling it out on a pitch set up on Port Ellen's sandy seafront.

Ride of the Falling Rain

Taking place in August (which has surprisingly high rainfall figures) this very informal 162-kilometre cycle ride around the island stops midway at Ardbeg distillery and raises funds for World Bicycle Relief, which does what it says on the tin.

Jura

'*Why does it take longer to get to Jura than it does to get to Peru?*', the labels on Jura's whisky bottles used to ask, answering, '*it just does*' – giving something of a flavour of the character of this large and largely empty island. Separated by only a narrow sound from Islay, Jura contrasts starkly with its neighbour in the way only Hebridean islands can. The population of only around 200 is strung along the forty-odd kilometres of its eastern coastline, and is vastly outnumbered by the 6,000 red deer which keep the interior of the island a rugged, tree-free moorland.

The usual access to Jura is a short hop on the tiny car ferry that plies to and fro across the sound from Port Askaig on Islay – itself a couple

of hours' ferry journey from Kennacraig on the Kintyre peninsula. The ferry lands at Feolin, at the southern end of Jura's road that links most of the eastern coast. During the summer months there is also a fast RIB that operates a passenger-only service from Tayvallich; this takes an hour and lands at Craighouse, Jura's main settlement. Here you'll find Jura's shop, cafe, hotel and distillery; there's also a bed and breakfast and a few holiday cottages.

Climb the Paps

Jura is dominated by three great cones of quartzite scree that rise like pyramids from the moor – the awe-inspiring Paps. The lack of paths and extreme steepness and ruggedness make the round of all three Paps one of the most challenging of Scotland's classic big hillwalks. The highest, Beinn an Oir ('the golden mountain'), is actually the easiest to climb, and can be done on its own. Starting from the bridge over the Corran River, wet and indistinct paths lead over the bogs to eventually cross the outflow of Loch an t-Siob. The route to Beinn an Oir then passes the north side of the loch before climbing to the bealach (or pass) between Beinn an Oir and its neighbour, Beinn Shiantaidh. From here a rising terrace heads up across the eastern side of the mountain before a final walk over angular quartzite stones leads up to the summit – an incredible viewpoint. The easiest return is to retrace your steps.

The full round of the Paps is only for the toughest of hill gangrels; for this, the route is the same as for Beinn an Oir as far as the outflow of Loch an t-Siob, but from there head north to reach the south-east ridge of Beinn Shiantaidh – and then embark on a gruelling battle with loose shifting screes to the summit. The descent of the west ridge also requires care before the terrace described above is used for the ascent of Beinn an Oir. From there, the descent is down the

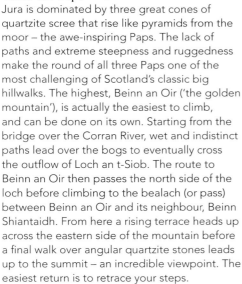

south ridge – but this is complex terrain where scree and boulders require very careful route finding. The final pap – Beinn a' Chaolais – looks particularly intimidating, and is best ascended (and descended) by heading around to the foot of its east ridge, before more bog trotting leads down to Loch an t-Siob. Be sure to leave enough time for a well-deserved dram at the hotel.

Experience the Jura Fell Race

If walking the Paps is too much, spare a thought for the fell runners who come to challenge themselves on the island's fearsome fell race. Held annually in late May, the race – a mad twenty-eight-kilometre tumble up and down the scree and heather clad slopes of not just the three main Paps, but four further summits – attracts entries from all over the globe. The winner arrives back at the hotel in Craighouse usually just over three hours after setting out – a quite incredible feat. Respect and bragging rights as well as an obligatory Isle of Jura whisky dram to all finishers, many of whom camp outside the hotel and make a long weekend out of the trip. If you want to compete you need to get in early; the race gains popularity every year with a ballot for successful entries taking place in January. Many fell runners come to Jura to test themselves against the Paps at other times of year. *www.jurafellrace.org.uk*

Ride the Corryvreckan whirlpool

Off the remote north coast of Jura, in the Gulf of Corryvreckan, is the third largest whirlpool in the world. There are a number of boat operators who will take you on a thrilling ride to experience it up close. The best times are during high spring tides when the underwater pinnacles cause maximum obstruction to the rushing tidal water between Jura and Scarba, which once led the Royal Navy to declare the strait 'unnavigable'. The author George Orwell

1 Jura, Beinn an Oir – highest of the Paps **2** Jura, otter

himself had a near miss in these waters and had to be rescued, along with his son, after their boat capsized and they were left clinging to a rock. The whirlpool can also look dramatic from the land at the right state of tide; it's a long day's walk along the rough track (no cars) from Ardlussa as far as Kinuachdrachd (look out for otters!) and then follow a final boggy moorland path above the coast to reach a viewpoint overlooking the narrows.

Face Room 101 at Barnhill

George Orwell came to Jura in 1946 seeking isolation and fresh air following the death of his wife and a bout of pneumonia. He stayed with his son Richard and housekeeper at remote Barnhill in the north-east of the island on and off until 1949 and wrote his dystopian classic *Nineteen Eighty-Four* there. Barnhill is now available to stay in as an off-grid self-catering holiday let. Walkers can peer down at it from the track from Ardlussa on their way to the Corryvreckan whirlpool.

Sample a dram

If it honestly takes longer to get here than to Peru, then you really ought to sample a dram. The Jura distillery runs friendly tours and produces a special bottling for its Tastival whisky festival held here in June to coincide with Fèis Ìle on Islay.
www.jurawhisky.com

Whisky purists may want to visit the source of the water. The walk to Market Loch is a moderate uphill hike alongside a tumbling burn, ending at the tranquil waters of the small loch which is also a popular fishing spot.

Laze on the sands at Corran

The beautiful strand of white sand and sheltered waters at Corran Sands makes this an ideal spot for a paddle on a warm day. Although it's by far the finest beach on Jura, the huge expanse of shell sand means it never feels busy. It was here that the islanders traditionally loaded their cattle on to boats to send them to market on the mainland. Many Diurachs left their island from this beach, bound for the New World during the years of famine and Clearances.

Investigate the story of Maclean's Skull with a bothy trip

Jura's west coast is extremely wild and rugged, but has two open bothies where you can stay and which make a number of mini-adventures possible. The red tin roof of Glengarrisdale is a welcome sight after the arduous boggy walk across the north-west of the island, with only the faintest of paths. A night here could also involve an exploration of Maclean's Skull Cave, followed by a spot of spooky storytelling in front of the bothy fire. The bothy itself sits just below a rocky crag said to be the site of a castle of Clan Maclean. A clan chief was slain here in a battle against the rival Campbells of Craignish, and his skull sat under an overhang just beyond the bothy for several centuries until the 1970s when it vanished. You may feel the hairs on the back of your neck rise up after a few drams by the fireside. There is also another bothy at Cruib on Loch Tarbert.

Jura Music Festival

Now well into its twenties, Jura's annual traditional music festival is held every September and has a laid-back vibe. It usually features an energetic ceilidh where you can dance the night away with local Diurachs, a concert in the distillery cooperage and further marquee-based events; festival camping is on the grass in front of the island's hotel.
www.juramusicfestival.com

1 Jura, Craighouse harbour   2 Jura, Barnhill   3 Jura, distillery   4 Jura, Evans' Walk
5 Jura, Glengarrisdale bothy   6 Jura, Corran Sands

Cross the island on foot

Jura is almost cut in half at its middle and here it is possible to walk from one coast to the other in a short, leisurely stroll. From the east coast at Tarbert Bay you can walk west along a track to a picturesque boathouse and a sea inlet on the island's east coast. Those looking to make a full day out of walking across the island can do so further south; Evans' Walk crosses the moors using a boggy and wild route, passing just north of Corra Bheinn to reach lonely Glenbatrick – a beautiful spot. Watch out for golden eagles on this route.

Colonsay

Colonsay is small enough to be explored by bike and on foot, yet large enough to keep you busy for at least a week – with spectacular beaches, rugged miniature hills and a vibrant community, it's a perfect microcosm of the best of the Hebrides.

The island is served by a CalMac vehicle ferry from Oban five times a week in the summer and four times in the winter; there's also a weekly ferry link to Port Askaig on Islay (enabling a day visit from its larger neighbour). The boats land at the tiny settlement of Scalasaig where there is a general store, cafe/bakery, bookshop, craft shop, village hall and bed and breakfast accommodation. The island's only hotel is just up the road. A few kilometres over hilly ground (bringing a bike or hiring one is a good option for getting around) brings you to Colonsay House, which has a cafe and gardens open to the public – there is also a nearby bunkhouse. There are self-catering accommodation options scattered across the tiny island.

Kiloran Bay and Traigh Ban

Kiloran Bay is a fabulous beach with custard-yellow sand and a reputation for waves, earning it the wild swimming title of the 'Colonsay washing machine'. Strong swimmers can test themselves in the bracing waters here. Others can walk along the track for five kilometres past Balnahard to reach the perfect white sands of Traigh Ban – this is usually more sheltered and provides secluded swimming and beachcombing.

Complete the whale sculpture ...

Just west of Kiloran Bay lies a 160-metre-long whale – not a beached carcass, but a massive art installation constructed as an outline in local stones by Julian Meredith in 2002. Since then, locals and visitors have been invited to add a stone, and the giant creature's outline is gradually being filled in. It has recently been recognised as an official landscape feature by the Ordnance Survey.

... and see it at its best

The whale sculpture is hard to appreciate from ground level – the best way to see it is to climb to the top of nearby crag Carnan Eoin. Topped by an impressive cairn overlooking Kiloran Bay, this is the highest summit on the island and Colonsay's finest viewpoint.

Bag the MacPhies

If just one hill isn't enough, Colonsay has its own 'mini Munros'. The MacPhies are twenty-two hills above 300 feet (ninety-one metres) that are dotted across the island. With much tough terrain, the challenge to complete them all in a day involves a gruelling thirty-two-kilometre hike. The record time to beat currently stands at just under four hours.

Drink in Colonsay's finest

Colonsay claims to be the smallest island in the world with its own brewery, which opened well before the recent boom in craft ales. It produces three very quaffable brews as well as special occasion bottlings. The brewery has recently been joined by a small distillery, as Wild Thyme Spirits are now producing Colonsay

1 Colonsay, Beinn nan Gudairean – a MacPhie **2** Colonsay, whale **3** Colonsay, Scalasaig **4** Colonsay, Kiloran Bay

gin, allegedly with the help of spirit helpers or 'brownies' who traditionally crop up in Celtic mythology, residing in people's houses and helping with the household chores.

Bee happy

Colonsay is one of the last places in the country where the Scottish native black honey bee is thriving under the custodianship of legendary beekeeper and oyster farmer Andrew Abrahams. Colonsay's black bees are the only ones thought to be isolated enough to prevent interbreeding with imported bees. They are now specially protected in law – it is an offence to bring other honey bees to Colonsay and Oronsay. Their very special honey can be sampled at the shop and cafe.

Ceòl Cholasa

Every September the village hall is buzzing with creative talent, both island-bred and from far afield, as Colonsay celebrates its music festival. Many people come year after year to enjoy and take part in the super-friendly folk-based concerts and ceilidhs, with further sessions in the hotel bar till the wee hours.
www.ceolcholasa.co.uk

Book festival

Taking place in April, this low-key literary event attracts top-name authors despite the remote location. Previous guests have included Alexander McCall Smith, A.L. Kennedy and Val McDermid.
www.colonsaybookfestival.org.uk

Oronsay

This small but fascinating island lies just off the southern shore of Colonsay. Crossing the tidal strip of exposed sand known as The Strand at low tide to visit Oronsay is a must. Check the tide times very carefully with locals as the crossing can be dangerous, and be sure to make the outward journey as early as possible during the falling tide. A bit of paddling will usually be required – and you may see the post office van splashing through the shallows to deliver to the island. Oronsay is home to eight people but there are no facilities for visitors.

Oronsay Priory
Be sure to visit the fourteenth-century ruined priory, complete with an ossuary where you'll see human skulls and bones. Outside stands a very fine carved Celtic cross. As long as you cross The Strand on a receding tide you should have time to walk to the priory, explore a little and visit one of the fine beaches and return to Colonsay before the tide cuts you off.

Hear the rasp of the corncrake
A relative of the moorhen, the corncrake was once widespread across Britain, but changes in farming practices saw its range shrink catastrophically until it remained on only a few Scottish islands – including here. Oronsay is farmed by the RSPB in a corncrake-friendly manner and you may well hear their unique rasping call on a visit in summer – they are notoriously difficult to see as they hide in the uncut grasses.

Gigha

This uncharacteristically fertile island lies four kilometres off the coast of the Kintyre peninsula, its green and verdant character lending it the nickname 'God's island'. Gigha had a succession of private owners before a buyout by the local community in 2002. The population has expanded since and although it hasn't all been plain sailing, new businesses have been developed and the future looks positive.

A regular CalMac vehicle ferry links Gigha to Tayinloan on the Kintyre peninsula, operating seven days a week. The jetty is at Ardminish, the main cluster of houses on the east coast of the island; the island's hotel is here, together with the shop, post office and an art gallery. There is around eight kilometres of quiet road from one end of the island to the other, making cycling or walking the ideal means of transport for visitors.

Climb Creag Bhan
Though only 101 metres high, this is the island's highest hill, its name translating as the White Rock. It's easily climbed by turning off the road on to a signed track at Druimyeon More. Keep right at a fork in the track and then look for a signpost indicating the start of the path to the top. From here the whole of Gigha can be seen, as well as Kintyre, the islands of Jura, Islay, Mull on a clear day and even Northern Ireland if you are blessed with perfect conditions.

See the gardens at Achamore House
These twenty-hectare gardens just a kilometre from the ferry jetty are run by the community. They contain a vast array of rhododendrons and azaleas collected by the former owner of the island – and inventor of the malted milk bedtime drink – James Horlick.

1 Oronsay, beach **2** Oronsay, post office van crossing the strand **3** Oronsay, Priory cross **4** Gigha, Creag Bhan

The Twin Beaches

It's well worth walking or cycling to the less-populated northern end of the island, passing a fine standing stone along the way. Climb up to the North Cairn for stunning views towards the Paps of Jura, and then head for the narrow isthmus that links Eilean Garbh to the rest of the island, with beaches on either side. The southern beach of Bagh Rubha Ruaidh is pleasant enough, but the real gem is north-facing Bagh na Doirlinne across the narrow dune-like spit; the fine sand here makes for a truly stunning spot.

Gigha music festival

This tiny, friendly traditional music festival attracts some fantastic bands and many of the best of Scotland's young musicians to Gigha towards the end of June. The 150-capacity village hall is usually crammed to bursting. Other events include a Piper's Picnic, a big ceilidh (the festival claims the record for the longest continuous Strip the Willow – sixty-five minutes), late-night sessions in the island's hotel, a barbecue and a last night survivors' concert.

www.gighamf.org.uk

Raft race

Usually held towards the end of July, this fun event is organised by the island's restaurant and sees teams racing an array of home-made rafts across the bay.

Cara

This small, uninhabited island is a kilometre south of Gigha, which would be the best place to try to find a boatman if you want to make a visit. It is said to be the only Scottish island still owned by a descendant of the Lords of the Isles (originally based on Islay), but the only inhabitants today are a herd of feral goats.

1 Gigha, view to Paps of Jura   **2 Gigha**, Twin Beaches

This chain of smaller isles stretches all along the Firth of Lorn into the outer reaches of Loch Linnhe. For hundreds of years the Slate Islands were the scene of heavy toil as their quarries were worked to produce over eight million slates a year, roofing much of Scotland. Today all is changed, the quarries long closed, the landscape quiet and peaceful, with many of the former workers' cottages serving as picturesque holiday homes. Further north, Kerrera provides an easily reached taste of alternative tourism for visitors to Oban, while Lismore is an unspoilt idyll which well deserves its Gaelic name, meaning 'the Big Garden'.

THE FIRTH OF LORN & LOCH LINNHE

Opposite Lismore, Castle Coeffin **Overleaf** Seil, coast near Ellenabeich, looking to Mull

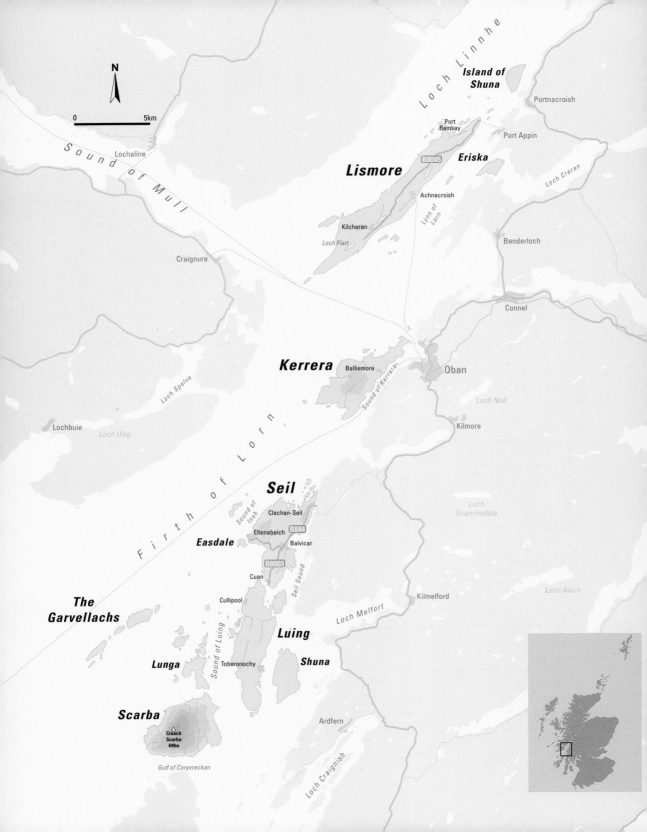

Seil

Set in the Firth of Lorn, Seil is the most northerly, populous and accessible of the Slate Islands, being linked to the mainland by a fine stone bridge since the late eighteenth century. Known as the 'islands that roofed the world', the economy of the group was dominated by slate production, though despite a quarry at Balvicar briefly reopening in the 1950s and 1960s the economy is now largely dependent on tourism. Seil has a choice of bed and breakfasts as well as self-catering accommodation, an inn and a couple of bars/restaurants; the main grocery shop is at Balvicar.

Cross the 'Bridge over the Atlantic'
While it could never live up to its grand nickname, the bridge more properly known as Clachan Bridge is certainly a magnificent structure. It dates back to 1792/3; originally intended by designer John Stevenson to have two arches, the plans were amended by Robert Mylne to include the single graceful arch that carries traffic over to Seil to this day. Next to it is an old inn, the Tigh an Truish (or House of Trousers). When kilts were outlawed in the aftermath of Culloden, Seil's residents would leave their kilts here before crossing to the mainland.

Discover Ellenabeich
Across the far side of the island is its picturesque capital of whitewashed former slate workers' cottages. The village was named after the island of Eilean-a-beithich which was just offshore, but was quarried away until nothing remained. Today Ellenabeich is a visitors' delight, but the livelihoods of villagers ended abruptly in 1881 when the sea broke into the main quarry pit – which had been worked to well below sea level – ending the industry here. The Scottish Islands Heritage Trust displays tell the sad story. If you're feeling energetic, the village is a great place to start a walk – either up grassy tracks to the north to visit the west coastal cliffs and their stunning views to Mull, or south-east along the coastline to the Luing ferry at Cuan.

See the stained glass at Kilbrandon Church
Just over a kilometre along the road from the Cuan ferry pier is this isolated church, its plain exterior dating back to 1866 when it replaced an earlier church in Cuan itself. It's well worth visiting for its striking stained-glass windows made by Douglas Strachan in 1937. The church can be included in a circular walk from Ellenabeich, following the coast to Cuan, along to the kirk and then back to the village over the moors; the route is mostly unmarked.

Easdale

Tiny Easdale is the smallest permanently inhabited island in the Inner Hebrides, and it must rank amongst the Scottish islands most comprehensively altered by man. The whole land area was heavily worked for slate, and away from the cottages its surface is completely pock-marked with old flooded pits and spoil. Now quiet, most visitors find it to be a slice of heaven. To reach it, a tiny but regular passenger ferry operates from Ellenabeich on Seil – carrying just ten people at a time. Easdale has a bar that doubles as a restaurant and tea room, and a bed and breakfast as well as several self-catering cottages.

Explore the village
While some of its picturesque cottages are inevitably holiday homes, Easdale's village is today home to around sixty people, having almost become completely deserted a few decades ago. The fact that there are no cars helps give it a truly special atmosphere, and

the first thing you'll notice when disembarking from the ferry is the multicoloured fleet of wheelbarrows that the locals use to transport goods and belongings to and from the boat. There's the 'Puffer bar' – which also serves as restaurant and tea room – and a tiny museum amidst the rows of whitewashed cottages, arranged around a central green and several old flooded quarry pits, all with great sea views. The beautifully modernised community hall is a great concert venue and has hosted some of Scotland's finest folk musicians.

Climb the wee summit

You might think that an island of less than ten hectares wouldn't have a walk worth the name, but you'd be wrong. Don't miss the chance to take a walk on old slate paths and across the great heaps of spoil over towards the western side of the island. A path climbs up to the highest point, and although just thirty-eight metres above the sea the outlook from the view indicator – both over Easdale and across the sea to the surrounding islands – is sensational on a fine day.

Take part in the World Stone-Skimming Championships

More than 300 people from around the world flock to Easdale each September to take part in this truly unique sporting event. Taking advantage of one of the old flooded quarries which makes for a perfect arena, and the plentiful flat, thin slate fragments, the world championships have been held here every year since 1997. Anyone can enter, and each contestant is allowed three skims. Throws are judged on distance, not the number of bounces, but to be a valid skim, the stone must bounce at least twice. With barbecue, craft stalls and a live music bash the preceding night, this is truly one of the quintessential Scottish island experiences.
www.stoneskimming.com

Luing

Viewed on a map, Luing is almost a twin to Seil, being a similar size and with the same history of slate quarrying. However, the lack of a bridge means it is much less visited than its better-known neighbour, and the population has declined to a couple of hundred. It takes just five minutes for the CalMac ferry to carry cars and passengers across the Cuan Sound between the two islands, and once over there's a store and post office on the road into Cullipool, a cafe at the Atlantic Islands Centre, a bed and breakfast and some self-catering cottages.

Walk the quarry coast

This rugged hike begins from the ferry pier, initially following a grassy track to Cuan Point. It then heads along the west coast all the way to Cullipool, passing through the main old slate quarrying areas. Some parts are boggy, and at one point the slate route has fallen into the sea, now requiring a detour down and across awkward boulders, submerged at highest tide and overshadowed by cliffs. The largest quarries are reached just short of Cullipool, where 150 workers would produce 700,000 slates a year; quarrying here continued until the 1960s. After exploring the village you can return the same way or continue round the quiet roads for the return to the ferry.

Catch a Cullipool sunset

Like Ellenabeich and Easdale, Cullipool is a beautiful cluster of old whitewashed stone slate workers' cottages, but it receives far fewer visitors. It's a sleepy place, little changed in decades, but recently the Atlantic Islands Centre has brought a new lease of life, with a cafe and exhibitions. If you can, it's worth staying in Cullipool to witness one of its memorable sunsets, sinking into the Firth of Lorn behind the Garvellachs and Mull.

Shuna

Lying in a sheltered position to the east of Luing, Shuna is green and richly wooded, with a single farm and a permanent population of just two people, though there are plenty of deer, seals and otters. The impressive ruined castle here was built in just 1911 as a private home, but it fell into ruin in the 1980s as it was too expensive to maintain. There is no regular ferry or boat trips to Shuna, but it is possible to hire one of several cottages for a week-long stay; the owners collect guests from nearby Arduaine on the mainland.

Lunga

On the opposite side of Luing is Lunga and its several smaller neighbours – Rubha Fiola (which is tidal), Eilean Dubh Mor and Eilean Dubh Beag, and Belnahua. Lunga was for many years used as an outdoor pursuits base but is now uninhabited; there is no regular boat service but it may be possible to visit the island by charter from Cullipool. The most northerly of the group, tiny Belnahua, was once a larger island, but it was slowly eaten away as it was quarried by its inhabitants, who once numbered almost 200; today it is deserted.

Scarba

The southernmost of the Slate Islands, Scarba is separated from Jura by the Gulf of Corryvreckan, famed for its great whirlpool (page 43), while another fearsome tidal race – the Grey Dogs – runs through the northern straits to Lunga. The island is wild and rugged, akin to Jura in character, rising like a squat pyramid to its highest point, Cruach Scarba, at 449 metres. There's some woodland on its eastern shores around Kilmory Lodge, but much of the interior is barren. Despite extending to over 1,400 hectares, Scarba has not been permanently inhabited since the 1960s, and is today used for grazing animals and occasional deer stalking. There is no regular boat access, but it may be possible to secure a charter at Craobh Haven, Crinan or Cullipool. The ascent to the Cruach is extremely tough going but the reward is with an unforgettable view.

The Garvellachs

This chain of small islands lies out to the west of the Slate Islands, the name Garvellachs coming from the Gaelic *An Garbh Eileaicha* – 'the Rough Islands'. While the largest is Garbh Eileach itself, the more southerly Eileach an Naoimh is the best known; it was the site of an early monastery founded by St Brendan of Clontarf in AD 542. Though abandoned by the ninth century, it became a centre of pilgrimage in the Middle Ages and its isolation has helped its preservation. The island is also renowned for its beehive-shaped double cell, which stands to a height of three metres. The ferry from Oban to Colonsay passes close to the islands, but there is no regular boat access. Landing trips can be arranged through Seafari on Easdale.

Kerrera

Extending for around seven kilometres in length, Kerrera is separated from mainland Argyll by its namesake Sound, providing the shelter that has made Oban into one of the most important ports in the West Highlands. There is a choice of ways to reach Kerrera,

1 **Scarba and the Garvellachs** from Luing 2 **Kerrera**, Gylen Castle 3 **Kerrera**, Hutcheson Monument 4 **Kerrera**, Gylen Castle

with the main regular passenger ferry making the short crossing from Gallanach, while a second ferry (booking required) runs from Oban itself to the marina at the north end of the island. Kerrera's tea garden also operates as a bunkhouse, while at the north end of the island a bar/restaurant serves the marina.

Complete the classic circuit with castle and cake

An eleven-kilometre loop around the southern half of Kerrera is possible from the Gallanach ferry pier, making for one of the classic walks of the southern Hebrides. A short detour from the track leads to the dramatic ruin of Gylen Castle on the southern coastline, which has been partially restored to allow you to climb to the top of the keep. The other unmissable feature of the circuit comes soon after, with a visit to the tea garden for hearty soup, home-made bread and delicious cake. It should be enough to power you through the boggy sections on the return leg of the walk.

Uncover CalMac's roots at the Hutcheson monument

This imposing obelisk can be reached by a five-kilometre (each way) walk from the Gallanach ferry, or much more quickly by using the marina ferry from Oban itself. The monument was built in 1883 to commemorate David Hutcheson, who set up the Burns shipping company that ran the first steamers on Scotland's west coast. His brother-in-law David MacBrayne extended the services, and although the days of the steamers are long gone, the company heritage continues into today's Caledonian MacBrayne (CalMac). Fittingly, the monument gives superb views of the almost constant stream of CalMac ferries heading into and out of the bay.

1 Lismore, Port Ramsay   **2** Lismore, ferry from Port Appin   **3** Lismore, Tirefour broch

Lismore

Set at the mouth of Loch Linnhe, Lismore is fifteen kilometres long but always less than two kilometres wide. Its name means 'Big Garden', which gives some impression of this verdant and fertile island, low-lying but surrounded by the hills and mountains of the mainland and Mull. There's a CalMac vehicle ferry that takes fifty minutes to cross from Oban to Achnacroish at the centre of the island, while the northernmost tip can be reached by a much shorter passenger-only ferry from Port Appin. Lismore has a choice of bed and breakfast and self-catering cottages, a bunkhouse and a campsite; there's also a small shop at Achnacroish.

Discover Port Ramsay

You'd struggle to find an island hamlet more picturesque, unspoilt and sleepy than little Port Ramsay, a string of terraced whitewashed cottages which once housed workers producing lime. It can be visited as part of an enchanting circular walk from the jetty served by the Port Appin ferry, initially following an unmarked route around the northern coastline and passing the old lime kilns before returning to the ferry along quiet roads.

Breach the defences of
Tirefour broch

Tirefour Castle is actually an Iron Age broch, the best preserved in all the Inner Hebrides, and it remained in use until well into the Middle Ages. Dating back two millennia, the defensive walls would once have stood to around fifteen metres in height, but they are still imposing, reaching almost five metres in places and being four and a half metres thick, with passageways inside. Set atop a grassy mound, the broch has a superb location still commanding grand views up and down the Lynn of Lorn. It can be reached by a walk of around three kilometres each way from Achnacroish.

Castle Coeffin

Once a stronghold of Clan MacDougall, the thirteenth-century ruins of Castle Coeffin still rise high from its rocky outcrop, though they are now heavily draped with ivy. Set right on the west coast of Lismore, the castle has great views across to Morven and along the coast to Achadun Castle; the walk to it starts from Clachan, near Lismore's main church.

Bike to Achadun Castle

Lismore's sleepy lanes and low-lying relief make it an ideal island for leisurely exploration by bike. You can take your two wheels across with you on the ferry from Port Appin and cycle the length of the island; one great objective is to bike as far as Mid Auchinduin and then follow a grassy track down to visit the ruins of Achadun Castle which have fine views across to Mull. In proper cycling tradition, cake at the Liosbeag Cafe is an essential stop on your way back; adjacent is a fine heritage centre and museum, including a faithful reconstruction of a cottar's house.

Eriska

This small island at the mouth of Loch Creran is best known for its luxurious hotel, its whole 120-hectare extent making up the grounds. The island is separated from the Benderloch peninsula by the tidal narrows of An Doirlinn, which are crossed by a road bridge – though only the vehicles of hotel guests are allowed.

Indulge yourself at a most opulent island retreat

The Isle of Eriska Hotel and Spa must rank amongst Scotland's most romantic retreats. Originally built as a grand family home, the hotel now offers five-star accommodation as well as a highly regarded fine dining restaurant. Sixteen of the thirty-four bedrooms are in the original house, which has a country house feel with open fires and oak panelled walls; Dame Judi Dench has been a guest, but you could imagine James Bond might choose to stay here too. **www.eriska-hotel.co.uk**

Discover Eriska's sculptures

If your budget doesn't stretch to the hotel, you can instead park at the Shian Wood car park, off to the right from the minor road to Eriska just before Balure of Shian. From here you can continue along the road and cross the bridge to the island on foot. Once on the island there is a network of informal paths – some signed, some not – that explore the whole of this magical oasis. Deserving of special note are some of the island sculptures – look out for Ronald Rae's abstract stone horse in the north of the island, or Kenneth Robertson's beautiful bronze otter further along the coast to the west.

Island of Shuna

Not to be confused with its namesake Shuna in the Slate Islands group, the Island of Shuna lies to the north of Lismore, separated from the mainland by the 300-metre-wide Sound of Shuna. There's a table-shaped hill towards the southern end, above Castle Shuna – the ruins of an old tower house. The island is two kilometres long and one kilometre wide, and there is no regular boat access.

1 Eriska, sculpture **2** Eriska, bridge **3** Eriska, hotel **4** Lismore, cycling

One of the bigger Scottish islands, Mull seems even larger as you try to navigate its narrow, twisting roads. The tall, multicoloured houses clustered around Tobermory's harbour have become one of Scotland's most recognisable views, but away from the capital the island is a wild and rugged place, celebrated for its white-tailed eagles, high mountains and endlessly convoluted coastline. Surrounding it is a whole series of diminutive neighbours, including probably Scotland's holiest isle – Iona, perhaps its strangest – Staffa, and the home of its friendliest puffins – Lunga.

THE ISLE OF MULL GROUP

Opposite Staffa, Fingal's Cave   **Overleaf** Mull, Traigh na Cille beach

N

0   5km

Kilchoan   Salen

Loch Sunart

Oronsay   *Carna*

Tobermory   Bunavullin

Loch Anenas

B8073   Dervaig
Calgary   Achnadrish
                                  Loch Frisa
Ensay   Ardnacross
                                        A848
Kilninian
        Fanmore
Lunga and the   Lochaline
Treshnish   Ballygown
Islands   B8073   Salen
                                        Pennygown
Gometra   Lagganulva   Kellan   Killiechronan
                  Killiemor   A849
Ulva   *Eorsa*   Gruline
                          Loch na Keal   Knock   Loch Bà   *Craignure*
Staffa *Little*   *Inch*   Derryguaig   Sgurr Dearg
          Colonsay *Kenneth*   Balnahard   Ben More   740m   Lochdon
                                            967m
Mull   B8035   A849
                                                      Strathcoil
                                              Ben Buie
                                              717m   Loch Spelve
                                  Beinn na Croise
Iona   Baile Mòr   503m   Loch Uisg
        Fionnphort   Torrans   Loch Scridain
                 A849   Loch Buie
        Bunessan
Erraid

Sound of Mull

Firth of Lorn

Sound of Iona

Loch Tuath

Mull

The second largest of the Inner Hebrides after Skye, Mull packs a weighty punch with the number of things to see and do. You could easily spend a couple of weeks exploring, or plan a number of mini-adventures or do a spot of wildlife watching. Mull has plenty of accommodation options from campsites to hotels, and all shops and facilities, although expect it to take longer than you might think to drive around the island's wiggly, mostly single-track, roads.

Three CalMac ferry routes cross to Mull. If coming from the south the most direct is from Oban, taking forty-five minutes to cross to Craignure. From the east or north check out the ferry from Lochaline to Fishnish which only takes fifteen minutes and is the cheapest option. There is also a ferry from Kilchoan in Ardnamurchan which takes thirty-five minutes. All three routes take vehicles; booking is recommended, especially on the very busy Oban–Craignure route. There's a regular long-distance coach service from Glasgow (and in the summer a direct bus links Glasgow airport with Mull) and there is a reasonable local bus service once on Mull so it is possible to plan a trip using public transport. Trains run to Oban from Glasgow, and Oban train station is conveniently located next to the ferry terminal.

Bag a Munro

Mull's highest peak, Ben More, is the only island Munro – or Scottish mountain over 3,000 feet high – outside of Skye. Standing at 966 metres above sea level, Ben More is often the mountain which baggers choose as their final Munro, due to it requiring a special trip to Mull and being a fairly accessible peak if non-mountain enthusiasts are joining the compleatist for the day. The quickest and easiest route is the up and down descent from Dhiseig which can be done in around five hours. An interesting and much more challenging ascent for more experienced mountain walkers takes you over the steep A'Chioch ridge with some rock scrambling and a real sense of accomplishment as you reach the top. Descending to Dhiseig makes a circuit out of it and leaves a fairly pleasant stretch along the coastal road at the end.

Taste a dram at Tobermory

Founded in 1798 and tucked away just off the seafront in Tobermory, the island's only distillery produces a range of single malts including a number of different barrel finishes and a forty-two-year-old which may or may not provide the answer to the meaning of life! Tobermory itself was established as a planned fishing settlement in 1788; before then there were just a number of farm buildings at the top of the hill. Not long afterwards a local kelp merchant, John Sinclair, leased the land at Ledaig and as soon as the ban on distilling was lifted in 1797 he built the distillery and began production. Its fortunes have ebbed and flowed with a forty-one-year closure following the depression of the 1930s and a number of shorter closures until the 1970s, but since the 1990s the distillery has expanded. There are a number of tours on offer, including tastings.
www.tobermorydistillery.com

Sample Mull's cheese

The Gulf Stream warmth combined with frequent rain and fertile soils make Mull a great place to produce milk and cheese. Isle of Mull Cheese is produced using traditional methods at Sgriob-ruadh farm just outside Tobermory. You can take a self-guided tour of the dairy farm and then sample the produce in the lovely glass-sided barn that houses the cafe and shop.
www.isleofmullcheese.co.uk

Experience Art in Nature

There could hardly be a more beautiful natural backdrop for the sculptures on this fascinating art walk. Either start at the stunning white sands of Calgary Bay and work your way up through the native woods, passing a number of stunning artworks including a large willow deer, or begin from the cafe where you can learn more about the project while refuelling on the home baking. *www.calgary.co.uk*

Adventure to the Fossil Tree

Venture into Mull's most remote wilderness on this long and very rough coastal walk (about a nineteen-kilometre round trip) on the Ardmeanach peninsula. The route is not for the faint-hearted and a whole day needs to be dedicated to the expedition. After a long approach and an airy traverse, the route leads down a rickety metal ladder for the final clamber along the shore. It's essential to time your arrival at this part for low tide. At the end you really do reach a geologist's dream.

Rising above you is the fossilised remains of an entire tree, a twelve-metre-high imprint embedded in the cliff face. Discovered in 1819 by John MacCulloch, it is known as MacCulloch's Fossil Tree and would have been engulfed by lava around sixty million years ago. The same eruptions would also have formed the amazing basalt columns that surround the tree along this section of coast. Waterfalls and a cave are added attractions on this walk, but don't underestimate just how tiring it is and bear in mind you'll need a head for heights and that the ladder is not possible with dogs.

Explore Mackinnon's Cave

Soaring cliffs provide the backdrop to the longest sea cave in the Hebrides. Once a showplace visited by Samuel Johnson and James Boswell, the cave is reached by a relatively short but arduous walk that can only be undertaken at low tide. From the parking area at Gribun walk past the farm at Balmeanach and eventually down on to the rocky foreshore, passing an impressive high waterfall. The cave itself is reached after a scramble over tidal boulders. A torch is handy for exploring the deep cave, although Johnson and Boswell had to make do with a candle in 1773. Legend has it that a piper was once lost in the depths of the cave with his dog. Eventually the dog re-emerged minus its hair but of the piper there was no sign and it is said that in certain sea conditions a piping lament can be heard along this coast.

See a sea eagle

No trip to Mull would be complete without a sighting of Britain's largest bird of prey. Your first encounter with the mighty sea – or white-tailed – eagle, may well be a swoosh in the sky above you as the bird's massive two-and-a-half-metre wingspan catches a thermal. Not for nothing are they known as 'flying barn doors'; these really are the kings of the air and once spotted you won't forget them. The RSPB runs Mull Eagle Watch, a hide-based experience with a guide which originally featured on BBC's *Springwatch* when the viewing public voted to name that year's chicks Itchy and Scratchy. There are many wildlife guides operating on the island and you also stand a good chance of spotting the birds on boat trips. Walking remote sections of the coast or in the mountains offers a great opportunity to catch sight of these birds which are much bigger than the golden eagle and much, much bigger than the buzzard. *www.mulleaglewatch.com*

1 Mull, Calgary art **2** Mull, Ben More **3** Mull, Tobermory **4** Mull, Fossil Tree **5** Mull, sea eagle **6** Mull, Mackinnon's Cave

Visit the Carsaig Arches

Mull has an embarrassment of natural rock arches, waterfalls and caves, but the Carsaig Arches and the tough walk to reach them make for a truly memorable day and should be a priority for any keen hikers visiting the island. While the walk itself requires a head for heights, even the drive down to the starting point at Carsaig pier is a not for the faint-hearted – a long descent on single-track road with very few passing places and a perilous steep drop at the side. The coastal walk passes a large cave supposedly previously inhabited by nuns cast out from Iona; nowadays it's more likely to house a feral goat or two – you'll smell them before you see them. The route out to Malcolm's Point and the arches becomes increasingly rough, although the first arch, surrounded by basalt columns and deep water at high tide, is ample reward. The classic view of the second arch is reached along a narrow clifftop path; the arch itself is topped by a chimney-like pinnacle.

Stroll to Tobermory's lighthouse

The walk out to Tobermory's lighthouse at Rubha nan Gall, Gaelic for 'stranger's point', is an absolute delight. To reach the start walk past the colourful properties of Tobermory's front towards the CalMac pier, turning off on a path to the left just after the RNLI centre. The path then weaves along the wooded cliff for two kilometres with tantalising glimpses of the hills of Ardnamurchan across the sea, sailing boats and the odd cruise liner between the trees. The point itself is a fantastic place to explore and watch for wildlife, particularly otters. The lighthouse was – like almost all in Scotland – built by the Stevenson lighthouse-building family, this one in 1857. Keepers and their families lived in the two cottages until the light was automated in 1960.

Round the crater loch

It's not every day that you get to climb a volcano. Although the hill of 'S Airde Beinn is long extinct, use your imagination to step back fifty-five million years to when Mull was a hotbed of volcanic activity. A short but steep

1 Mull, crater loch   **2** Mull, Duart Castle   **3** Mull, Calgary Bay ice cream shack

and boggy walk takes you right round the caldera of the volcano, with a lochan now filling the crater. The route starts just a few kilometres from Tobermory next to a ruined house on the Dervaig road. Climbing fairly steeply the path leads to the highest point, which despite being only 295 metres above sea level has fine views. You can continue all the way around the rim of the crater or descend to dip a toe in the lochan before returning back to the start.

Explore Duart Castle

You can't miss this impressive defensive pile as the ferry glides into Craignure. Set on a rocky outcrop projecting into the Sound of Mull, the castle has a fantastic strategic outlook over the Firth of Lorn, the Sound of Mull and Loch Linnhe. The original structure dates back to the thirteenth century, but much of what you can see today is the result of a major restoration in the twentieth century following a long period as a ruin. Home to Clan Maclean, you may recognise some parts from the 1999 film *Entrapment* (starring Sean Connery who claims Maclean ancestry), and the castle also had a

role in some of the *Buffy the Vampire Slayer* TV series (no Maclean ancestry as far as we know). The castle itself is open from March to October but the grounds can be explored year round. ***www.duartcastle.com***

See the white sand of Calgary Bay or dark sand of Traigh na Cille

Calgary Bay is one of the finest beaches on Mull, with a fine expanse of white sand, informal camping area, superb ice cream shack and lovely clear water. Best enjoyed at dawn or dusk when you can appreciate the wild setting, it's the perfect beach to launch a kayak from and paddle about the bay. However, it can become ever-so-slightly busy in midsummer (that's more than five people and a dog roaming the sands), so if it's solitude you're after, check out Traigh na Cille. Here black volcanic sand provides a stunning contrast to Calgary and you're likely to have this small bay all to yourself. Walk down the track heading to the shore from the bridge over the Allt na Cille near Kilninian on the Dervaig to Gruline road.

Try a taste of Mull

There's usually a small queue at the Fishermen's Pier fish and chip van on Tobermory's harbourfront. It's not only hungry humans and seagulls hanging around; the local otter population is also in the know and you may well be rewarded with a sighting of this elusive mammal swimming in the harbour or even wandering about amongst the creels on the pier or the nearby marina pontoons.

If you've deep pockets and want to sample the best of local produce, then the Ninth Wave restaurant at Fionnphort near the ferry to Iona is the place to eat. Locally grown veg is coupled with super-fresh seafood caught from the owner's boat, Mull-reared meat and venison, and imaginative desserts. Only open in the evenings between May and October, this is a serious adult eatery for a special treat.

See a show at Mull Theatre

Once the smallest professional theatre in the world, Mull Theatre company until recently produced and performed plays in a tiny converted cow byre at Dervaig. Now installed in a purpose-built theatre just outside Tobermory, the company has kept its reputation for innovative, high-quality and accessible performances. Catch it when you can, as the company is known for regularly being on the move and since it was established in 1966 it has performed in over 300 venues across the Highlands and Islands, playing to over a quarter of a million people, often in remote village halls.

1 **Iona,** Abbey 2 **Iona,** beach at Camas Cuiln an t-Saimh 3 **Iona,** view from Dun I 4 **Iona,** pier

Iona

It may be small, but Iona has a special place in the hearts of many Scots – and those from far beyond. Known as the cradle of Christianity in Scotland, the original monastery here was founded in the sixth century by St Columba, a monk who had been exiled from Ireland, and over the following centuries it became a great centre of culture and learning.

Iona is just a four-minute ferry ride from Fionnphort on Mull; cars can only be taken by residents, so you'll have to explore the island on foot or by bike. Coaches run day trips from Oban which can be a hassle-free and economical way to visit the island if you don't have time to also explore Mull. There are a number of accommodation options on Iona including a campsite, hostel, bed and breakfast, and two hotels, as well as a smattering of self-catering cottages. The two hotels offer food, as does the Martyr's Bay Restaurant situated right at the pier and specialising in local seafood. There are a couple of shops and bike hire.

Climb Dun I

The great thing about Iona is that its size (approximately one to two kilometres wide and six kilometres long) makes it perfect for exploring on foot, and heading up its highest hill is a great way to start. Head north along the road passing the abbey and eventually a row of white cottages. Turn left after these to climb rough ground following wooden waymarkers to the summit of Dun I (pronounced Ee). It may be small, topping out at just a single metre over a hundred, but it's a superb viewpoint and the cairn and trig point on the site of an Iron Age fort make it feel like a summit of significance. From here you can see the white sands of Traigh an t-Suidhe at the far north of the island, often busier with seaweed-munching cattle than people.

Be a pilgrim for the day at Iona Abbey

To many people, Iona – or *I Chaluim Chille*, 'Iona of St Columba' in Gaelic – means the abbey, and a visit is a personal pilgrimage. Originally a monastery founded by Columba in AD 563 following his exile from Ireland, over the centuries it became known as a place of religious learning and art. Many stone carvers spread around the country from here and Iona is thought to have been the centre where the beautifully illustrated *Book of Kells* was produced. The now restored abbey buildings house the ecumenical Iona Community, founded in response to what many saw as a failure of the traditional churches to respond to poverty particularly in west Scotland in the 1930s. You can stay with the community which also operates an adventure centre for young people.

South end beaches and the spouting cave

Iona's wildest landscapes are found at the south-west end of the island. Visit on a stormy day and you'll see water jetting high above a blowhole cave as the waves force seawater up through a large hole in the roof of the sea cave. The safest place to view this phenomenon is from the beach at the brilliantly named Camas Cuil an t-Saimh – 'Bay at the Back of the Ocean' – which itself is the perfect spot to spend an afternoon picnicking or beachcombing. To reach it head left along the road from the ferry and eventually aim westwards across Iona's golf course to reach the sandy machair at the back of the beach. From here you can continue across country via Loch Staoineig to the beach where St Columba is said to have landed when he first arrived from Ireland.

Snack at Heritage Garden Cafe

Relax at the picnic tables in the garden of the old manse and enjoy a cuppa and home-made cake or a toasted sandwich. The Heritage Centre can be found next to the historic church, designed by Thomas Telford, just to the right as you get off the ferry. The garden cafe is a peaceful oasis that feels hidden away even when Iona is busy with day trippers.

Erraid

There is something truly special about walking across the soft, sea-rippled sandy strait that separates Erraid from Mull. Or if you have a kayak you can land at the bay where David Balfour came ashore having been shipwrecked in Robert Louis Stevenson's novel *Kidnapped*. Erraid has been home to members of the Findhorn Foundation for over forty years; the residents aim to live as ecologically sustainable a life as possible while practising their spiritual values – overnight guests are welcomed by arrangement.

If crossing by foot check the tide times and aim to cross about an hour after high tide to give maximum time on the island before the return crossing becomes impassable.

Send a message to Skerryvore

Climbing to Erraid's high point, Cnoc Mor, is a must. Standing a mere seventy metres above sea level, the climb on a track and then a path is surprisingly tough. The view takes in all the tiny islets around Erraid as well as Iona and much of Mull. On the way back down be sure to detour to the small white rocket-like building. This originally served as a relay station for sending messages to Skerryvore lighthouse over forty-five kilometres out at sea and another nearer, offshore light. Built by Alan Stevenson,

his nephew Robert Louis spent much time as a child on the island and was inspired by the landscape when he came to write *Kidnapped*.

Ulva

Ulva is Scotland's newest community-owned island. Purchased in 2018, the island now belongs to the North West Mull Community Woodland Company. The island is reached by a short passenger ferry ride from Ulva Ferry on Mull; there is a community bus service to this point and also a car park. Summon the ferry by uncovering the red panel at the pier building – the ferry runs Monday to Friday, Easter to October, and on Sundays during high summer; in the winter the ferry runs to accommodate school times so it's best to check beforehand.

Dine at the Boathouse

Overlooking the ferry landing pier, The Boathouse can be a place of refuge on a foul weather day, or a welcome spot to sit outside and wait for the ferry while sampling the local seafood and home baking. The food is truly delicious, the welcome genuinely friendly and the setting unforgettable – even if you don't make it further than The Boathouse your visit to Ulva should count as a success.
www.theboathouseulva.co.uk

Overnight in a private bothy

Once home to over 850 people at the height of the kelp boom in the 1840s, Ulva's population plummeted following a combination of potato famine, a crash in the kelp market and then a brutal new owner who ruthlessly cleared many of the people from their cottages to make way for sheep. Within a few years of Francis Clark taking over as laird, over two thirds of the island's population had left, many of them

1 Erraid, beach 2 Ulva, The Boathouse cafe 3 Ulva, coast 4 Ulva, bothy

driven nearly to starvation. Accounts of their brutal treatment were relayed to the Napier Commission set up by the government to investigate the grievances of the crofters – evidence that Clark himself did nothing to refute. Clark was unusual in that he tended not to use a middle man or factor to enforce his evictions, preferring to do so himself even to the point of burning the thatch over people's heads to drive them from their homes. These days one of those homesteads at Cragaig is now a bothy where you can stay for the night by arrangement; it's a great destination for a walk and you can still make out the ruins of other houses. Records show that in 1841, fifty-seven people lived in this small settlement.

Gometra

Gometra is linked to Ulva by a bridge – and by a finger of land at low tide – a long walk from the Ulva's ferry jetty. The summit of the island, also known as Gometra, is classed as a Marilyn – a summit with a drop of 150 metres or more on all sides. Once home to a population high of 160 people, Gometra now has two permanent households and another with members who live on the island part-time. The island is privately owned and farmed; there are two basic bothies which can be booked for visitor stays.

Inch Kenneth

Lying to the south of Ulva is tiny Inch Kenneth, named after the saint who, as a follower of Columba, founded a monastery there. There is no regular access to Inch Kenneth without your own boat, but it is possible to make arrangements with local boat trip operators to be dropped off and picked up the same day, which will give you a few hours to explore the island. Alternative Boat Hire Iona can also arrange sailing trips in their boat the *Birthe Marie*, and Mull Charters runs trips during the summer months.

Circumnavigate the island on foot

Green and grassy Inch Kenneth provides easy walking and its small size makes it easy to explore on foot, with a number of sandy beaches for a break. Take in the eleventh-century chapel with its collection of delicately carved gravestones dating from between 1300 and 1500; several ancient Scottish kings are said to be buried on the island. The large ornate white house stands out against the green landscape and still gives the island an air of notoriety due to its association with the Mitford family, a number of whom were Nazi supporters, who bought the island in 1938. Unity Mitford was a friend – and some have claimed lover – of Adolf Hitler, and she attempted suicide in Germany by shooting herself in the head after Britain declared war in 1939. Hitler aided her return to the UK, and she lived on the island – damaged by her self-inflicted wound – until she died in Oban in 1948. The island eventually passed to Jessica Mitford, an ardent communist who fought in the Spanish Civil War, before being sold to the current owners in 1967. Nowadays the island is populated only by sheep.

Little Colonsay

This small green island lying between Ulva and Staffa was once home to sixteen people before the island was cleared by Francis Clark at the same time as the clearances on Ulva and Gometra. Now privately owned, just one large house remains habitable.

1 Staffa, path to Fingal's Cave **2** Little Colonsay **3** Gometra

Staffa

Named by the Vikings for the amazing basalt columns that reminded them of the logs their houses were made from, Staffa is a geological, bird-rich wonder. Reaching it requires a boat trip from either Ulva Ferry or Tobermory on Mull, or Kilchoan on the Ardnamurchan peninsula – these are popular and can book up weeks in advance in the summer months. The intrepid and experienced can make it to the islands by kayak or sturdier craft, but Staffa and the Treshnish archipelago are quite a way out in open water and reaching them is a serious expedition. Many of the boat trips offer landing options with some also stopping at neighbouring Lunga.

See Fingal's Cave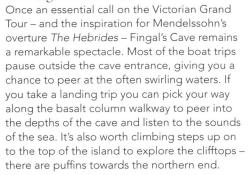

Once an essential call on the Victorian Grand Tour – and the inspiration for Mendelssohn's overture *The Hebrides* – Fingal's Cave remains a remarkable spectacle. Most of the boat trips pause outside the cave entrance, giving you a chance to peer at the often swirling waters. If you take a landing trip you can pick your way along the basalt column walkway to peer into the depths of the cave and listen to the sounds of the sea. It's also worth climbing steps up on to the top of the island to explore the clifftops – there are puffins towards the northern end.

Lunga and the Treshnish Islands

North-west of Staffa lie the eight main islands that make up this archipelago, often clearly visible from the coast of Mull, with numerous islets dotted in between. Uninhabited today, the islands contain evidence of being populated as far back as the Iron Age, with the remains of ancient hill forts, medieval chapels and other buildings being uncovered.

The largest island, Lunga, was inhabited until 1824 and is the easiest to visit – the others having very limited landing spots. A number of regular organised boat trips land here during the summer months, many of them offering the chance to combine Lunga with a trip to Staffa the same day.

Bac Mòr – also known as 'the Dutchman's Cap' – is the most distinctive island in the group, its name referring to its flat shape which surrounds a prominent dome. Its smaller sibling Bac Beag lies just to the south-west. The group's most northerly islands, Cairn na Burgh Beag and Cairn na Burgh Mor, share the defensive features of Cairnburgh Castle, the ruins of which are visible from passing boats on

1 Staffa, Fingal's Cave **2** Treshnish Islands, shag **3** Treshnish Islands, puffins

the larger isle. A matching guard house sits on the smaller isle, and both defend the entrance to Loch Tuath.

Puffins on parade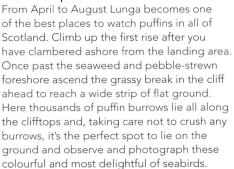

From April to August Lunga becomes one of the best places to watch puffins in all of Scotland. Climb up the first rise after you have clambered ashore from the landing area. Once past the seaweed and pebble-strewn foreshore ascend the grassy break in the cliff ahead to reach a wide strip of flat ground. Here thousands of puffin burrows lie all along the clifftops and, taking care not to crush any burrows, it's the perfect spot to lie on the ground and observe and photograph these colourful and most delightful of seabirds.

See Harp Rock stack

Stuffed full of nesting kittiwakes, guillemots, shags and razorbills, this rocky stack provides a real spectacle for birdwatchers. Only a fifteen-minute walk from the landing bay on Lunga, you will smell the rock before you come upon it. The path is clear but narrow and care should be taken around the cliffs nearest to the harp-shaped sea stack.

Eorsa

A small island lying in the middle of Loch na Keal, Eorsa is uninhabited except for sheep. It was used as an anchorage by the navy during the Second World War and can be visited by kayak or small boat.

Carna and Oronsay

Carna and its heavily indented neighbour Oronsay are situated in Loch Sunart, south of Glenborrodale. Carna is the larger and taller of the two islands and its position almost blocks Loch Sunart, creating two narrows, or kyles, that can present a real challenge to passing sailors and kayakers at certain tides. The island is home to a wildlife conservation project and it is possible to visit on certain days or stay as a self-catering guest; kayakers and others under their own steam can land on the island.

Neighbouring Oronsay is a tidal island but approaching by kayak is your best bet as a thick slick of muddy, treacherous ground needs to be crossed to access the island at low tide.

The most remote of the Inner Hebrides, low-lying and blessed by long hours of spring sunshine and unmatched beaches, Coll and Tiree appear at first to be twins, but that's not the whole story. Tiree is fertile and heavily crofted, its few hills enhanced in stature by the almost flat terrain of the rest of the island. Coll, on the other hand, is rugged and sparsely inhabited away from its tiny capital, Arinagour.

Just to the north are the Small Isles, which are even more varied. Rum has jagged rocky mountains; Canna is verdant green with a stunning coastline; Muck is a peaceful oasis; and Eigg has the unmistakeable Sgùrr, a dramatic history and an inspiring community.

COLL, TIREE
& THE SMALL ISLES

Opposite Laig Bay and the Cuillin of Skye, from the Sgùrr of Eigg   **Overleaf** Tiree, the Maze

Tiree

The most westerly of the Inner Hebrides, Tiree is renowned for its long hours of sunshine in the spring and early summer. The fertile soils here have helped Tiree retain a healthy population of around 650 people, many of them living in whitewashed cottages with tall, hipped roofs – a distinctive Tiree style known as a *Blacktop*. The island's Gaelic name *Tir fo Thuinn* means 'the Land Beneath the Waves', a reference to its flatness; this gives the wind free rein, and Tiree has become a centre for windsurfing.

Tiree is served by CalMac vehicle ferries from Oban which also call at the Isle of Coll en route; the ferries can be heavily booked in the summer season. There are also flights from Glasgow on Loganair, and twice a week from Oban (and Coll) operated by Hebridean Air Services. The island has shops and all types of accommodation including a hostel and campsite.

Find your way to the Maze

Tiree is justly famed for its beaches of finest white sand, which extend around a substantial part of its coastline. All are splendid, but if we had to choose just one it would be Traigh Thodhrasdail on the west coast – commonly known to windsurfers as 'the Maze'. On a fine summer's day it is heaven, while when the westerly wind gets up, the breaking waves can be truly spectacular. There's parking near Greenhill, from which it's a kilometre or so to walk along the shore.

Climb Carnan Mor

Tiree has a reputation for being flat, and it's true that most of the island is level and low-lying. However, there are three prominent hills rising from its western coastline, each of which provides a bird's-eye view over these fertile grassy fields fringed by beaches and sea. At 141 metres and topped by a radar station, Carnan Mor is the highest; it can be easily reached along a tarmac lane up the western flank, or cross-country from Hynish.

Sound the Ringing Stone

This massive boulder on Tiree's northern shore is balanced on top of smaller rocks and makes a metallic sound when struck gently by another rock – but take care not to cause damage. The surface of the rock has many cup markings thought to have been made by the Beaker people who lived here around 4,500 years ago. It is not related to local geology and was probably deposited here from the Isle of Rum by a glacier during the Iron Age, though local legend says it was thrown by a giant on Mull. The stone can be reached by following a track from near Gott across to the north coast, then following the coastline eastwards, or from Vaul by following the coast west from Dun Mor broch.

Experience the wilds of Ceann a' Mhara

The far western headland of Ceann a' Mhara is this gentle island's most rugged corner. There's a parking area at Meningie, and the superb beach of Traigh Bhi at Balephuil Bay provides a perfect approach to the peninsula. Aim for the scant ruins of St Patrick's Chapel then keep above the increasingly dramatic coastline to ascend by a fence line to the summit of Beinn Ceann a' Mhara – with superb views over the beaches on either side as well as out to Skerryvore lighthouse.

1 Tiree, Ceann a' Mhara **2** Tiree, Ringing Stone **3** Tiree, Traigh Bhi from Carnan Mor

Uncover the story of Skerryvore

Scotland's tallest and most spectacular lighthouse, and often claimed to be the most graceful in the world, Skerryvore marks a treacherous reef in a very remote position some seventeen kilometres south-west of Tiree's shores. The slender forty-eight-metre-tall tower is well seen from the island's hills and western coast on a fine day. The remarkable story of how the tower was built can be discovered at the Skerryvore Museum, housed in the complex of buildings at Hynish that served as the lighthouse's land station. Here are the lighthouse keepers' cottages for when they were off shift, a signal station for communication with the lighthouse, and a picturesque harbour. Tiree Sea Tours run trips out on a RIB for a closer look at this iconic tower.

Munch a lobster baguette

Seafood doesn't get any fresher than straight off Frazer MacInnes' boat at Scarinish harbour. As well as supplying oysters, langoustines and scallops – and local meats – Frazer has a trailer where you can buy a lobster or crab baguette to munch with your cup of tea as you sit by the bay – does life get much better than that?

Get into surf culture at Tiree Wave Classic

For a week every October, Tiree plays host to the world's longest-running professional windsurfing event. Spectators can experience the very best of wave culture, with social events through the week; you can also try out surfing, windsurfing and paddleboarding for yourself.
www.tireewaveclassic.co.uk

Tiree Music Festival

Founded by a musician from renowned Tiree-based band Skerryvore, Tiree's annual music festival has grown to become one of Scotland's best-known smaller festivals. The TMF is usually held each July and run by the local community. Numbers are limited to a maximum of 2,000 for a very special event with some of the best bands from across the Gàidhealtachd, Scotland and beyond.
www.tireemusicfestival.co.uk

Tiree Agricultural Show

An altogether more placid event, the agricultural show is one of the few in the Hebrides and is held in July. It's a real chance to get a peep into local island culture, with prizes for best cattle, sheep, poultry, tractors and even pets. There are demonstrations to watch, stalls to browse and the day's events draw to a close with the tossing of the sheaf! It's all rounded off with the obligatory evening ceilidh.

Coll

A casual glance at a map suggests that Coll may be a twin to its neighbour Tiree, but while it's a similar size, Coll is an island of a quite different character. Although it's low-lying, the landscape here feels far more wild and rugged, with fewer roads and less than half the population. The white shell sands which surround the island are stunning.

Coll is served by the same CalMac vehicle ferry from Oban that continues on to Tiree; the ferries can be very busy and get booked up in the summer season. There are also flights which operate twice a week from Oban, also landing at Tiree. Coll has a general store as well as the T.E.S.Co shop (The Ethical Sales Company), a cafe, hotel, bed and breakfast, bunkhouse, campsite and cottages to rent; all facilities are at Arinagour.

1 Coll, Hogh Bay   **2 Tiree**, boats at Loch Bhasapoll   **3 Tiree**, Hynish signal station   **4 Coll**, Feall Bay

1 **Coll**, Breachda Castles with distant Mull   2 **Coll**, hotel   3 **Coll**, Ben Hogh   4 **Coll**, Sorisdale
5 **Coll**, corncrake **Photo:** David Main   6 **Coll**, the road to the north-west   7 **Coll**, north-west coast

See the Breachacha castles

These two spectacular castles were once the seats of the Macleans of Coll. The older of the two is a fifteenth-century tower house set right on the island's shores; it was replaced by the impressive Georgian pile built further inland in the 1750s. Both of the castles are now private residences with no public access, so do respect the owners' privacy and keep out of their garden grounds.

Traigh Feall and Chrossapol

These two wonderful beaches are the largest on Coll, lying on either side of the narrowest part of the island. Feall Bay to the north and Crossapol Bay to the south make for a grand thirteen-kilometre circular walk, especially if combined with an exploration of the Calgary Point peninsula beyond. It's also worth ascending little Ben Feall nearby for an aerial view over this beautiful landscape.

Reach far Sorisdale

The long, narrow strip of road that runs to the northern end of Coll is ideal for cycling. It terminates just short of the former crofting and fishing community of Sorisdale. While a few houses here have been restored, most of the buildings are abandoned, their old thatched roofs collapsing. This is an atmospheric place to ponder on the past challenges and future of island life. Just beyond – as goes without saying on Coll – is a fine sandy beach, while faint paths northwards lead to the massive dunes that back Traigh Tuath.

Hear the call of the corncrake

Corncrakes were once a common bird through much of Britain, but the decline of uncut meadows has seen the population collapse. Today it hangs on, predominantly on only a few remote islands, and the RSPB reserve at Totronald is one of the few remaining strongholds. The birds are very seldom seen as they hide amongst the long grasses, irises and nettles, but listen during the summer months for their unmistakable rasping call, which sounds like the teeth of a wooden comb being stroked. There's also – you guessed it – a wonderful beach on the reserve, Traigh Hogh.

Visit the Queen's Stone on Ben Hogh

Ben Hogh is the only hill on Coll to top 100 metres in height, though the impression that gives of a flat island is belied by the reality of the landscape, which has many rocky mountains in miniature. Ben Hogh itself is well worth climbing, revealing superb views across the whole island. Near the summit is the Queen's Stone, a dramatic erratic boulder deposit by an Ice Age glacier atop three much smaller stones. The easiest ascent is from Clabhach, starting on a grassy track but rough and pathless towards the top.

Find your own secret cove on the north-west coast

While Coll has some magnificent wide sweeps of beach, probably its greatest sandy delights are found in the many tiny coves of perfect sand cradled amongst the rocks all along its north-western coastline. For several kilometres either side of the Iron Age fort of Dun Morbhaidh you can explore and find your own slice of perfection.

Be a greedy gannet

Coll has only one hotel, but it has a great reputation, having been run by the same family since the 1960s. The bar here is the heart of the local community, while the Gannet restaurant overlooking the harbour is renowned for its superb freshly caught seafood. Everything is made on site, right down to the burger rolls and spaghetti. ***www.collhotel.com***

Gaze at the Milky Way

The first island to be awarded Dark Sky status, and one of only a few official sites in Scotland, care has been taken to reduce light pollution from the few settlements on Coll. Observing the skies here on a clear night is a humbling experience – particularly in winter. The Milky Way can be seen in all its glory with around 6,000 stars visible to the naked eye on a good night.

Look for basking sharks

The second-largest fish in the world, basking sharks can grow to twelve metres in length and weigh up to nineteen tonnes. Present throughout the Hebrides, the seas off Coll are regarded as a particular hotspot in summer. Basking sharks feed on plankton, their huge mouths able to filter vast quantities of water as they swim just below the surface with their often floppy dorsal fin and tail visible above. You might be lucky enough to see one from the shore or the ferry; boat operator Basking Shark Scotland offers one-day tours from Coll (advance booking needed) that can even give the chance to swim with these great beasts of the ocean.

www.baskingsharkscotland.co.uk

Eigg

Even by Hebridean standards, Eigg is a special island. The most populated – though not the largest – of the magical Small Isles, it has a striking appearance, dominated by the improbable rock peak of An Sgùrr. The whole

island is packed with interest and history, running right up to modern times when the islanders themselves finally took on ownership after years living under absentee landlords. Eigg's community has a green ethos and has developed its own renewable energy. Eigg has its main shop and cafe near the ferry pier at Galmisdale, and there is a variety of accommodation here, including self-catering cottages, a bunkhouse, a bed and breakfast, private bothies to rent, wooden wigwams and yurts.

Eigg is served by CalMac's Small Isles ferry from Mallaig on a complex timetable that takes in a different combination of islands in a different order each day; only residents are allowed to bring vehicles over. During the summer months there is also a regular passenger service on the *M.V. Sheerwater* from Arisaig.

Climb the Sgùrr

A first glimpse of An Sgùrr can make you doubt the evidence of your own eyes. This massive block of pitchstone lava was the result of one of the final eruptions of a volcano whose core now forms the nearby island of Rum. The lava filled a glen and solidified, and the surrounding rock later eroded away to leave this inverted landscape. It looks impregnable, but a rough unmarked hill path from Galmisdale forks off from the Grulin track and heads round the northern side before climbing up to a bealach west of the summit. From here the highest point can be reached with a short rocky scramble; the views are unforgettable.

Explore the Massacre and Cathedral caves

These two fascinating caves on the southern coast of Eigg are reached by a track and then a rough path – partly waymarked in purple – from Galmisdale. From where the path reaches the coast, the Cathedral Cave can be reached by heading along the shore to the west but only if the tide is out. The massive entrance and roomy interior are said to have been used for Catholic services after the 1745 rebellion. Along the shore to the east is the much smaller entrance of the Uamh Fhraing (Cave of Frances) – better known as the Massacre Cave. This can be carefully explored if you have a torch; after a narrow passage it soon broadens to a roomy interior around seventy metres long. The story of the cave is a grim one; 395 islanders – Macdonalds – were killed here during a clan feud when the Macleods from Skye lit a fire to suffocate those hiding inside. Later the Macdonalds carried out a revenge massacre of the Macleods at Trumpan Church on Skye.

Watch the sunset from Laig Bay

Laig Bay is Eigg's largest beach, almost a kilometre of sand facing west towards the mountains of Rum, and the mix of sand colours here often form beautiful patterns. A visit at sunset can be an experience to remember as an orange sky silhouettes the jagged mountains across the sea, often reflected on the wet surface of the sand. The bay is a short walk from Cleadale in the northern part of Eigg; it can also be reached by a longer trip from Galmisdale, or by bike – cycle hire is available near the pier.

See the Finger of God

The rocky escarpment of Sgorr an Fharaidh in northern Eigg is little known and visited, but for the discerning visitor it provides a memorable hillwalk and a great alternative to the more popular An Sgùrr. A tiny unmarked path heads up from just south of the road fork in Cleadale; this peters out before the plateau is reached, but once atop the escarpment a grand walk heads northwards along the clifftops before

---

1 Eigg, the Finger of God **2** Eigg, Cathedral Cave **3** Coll, Basking shark **Photo:** Shane Wasik, *Basking Shark Scotland*
4 Eigg, the Sgùrr from Galmisdal

descending from Dunan Thalasgair in the north. Along the way is a rock pinnacle known as 'the Finger of God', which provides a dramatic foreground to a view over the bays to Rum.

Make the Singing Sands sing

Camas Sgiotaig beach at the north end of Cleadale has an outlook that rivals that from Laig Bay. In dry weather the grains of quartzite sand make a rasping or singing sound as you scuff your feet on them, or even when blasted by the wind. The bay can be reached by either of a couple of paths from each of the road ends in Cleadale; the two routes make for a good circuit but as usual a map is required.

Discover the Kildonan beaches

If you don't have time to reach the beaches on the northern half of Eigg, Kildonan near Galmisdale offers an alternative. The bays east of the old pier are attractive and give good views of the Sgùrr, but it's worth following the path above Poll nam Partan to meet the track to Kildonan Farm before heading south towards the point for the finest beach in southern Eigg. While in the area make sure you head to the ruins of Kildonan Kirk just north-west of the farm to see the remains of a very fine carved Celtic cross.

Dine at Eigg's cafe

The cafe/restaurant at Galmisdale Bay – in the same building as the shop – is yet another great reason to visit the island. It serves home-made burgers and as good a bowl of local Arisaig mussels as you'll find anywhere, accompanied by hand-cut chips. If you score one of the tables on the terrace then the view out over the sea isn't too shabby either.
www.galmisdale-bay.com

Dance at the Anniversary Ceilidh

Eigg was owned by a string of private landowners over many years, and in 1995 was sold to an eccentric German artist known as Maruma. By 1996 it was on the market once again and many of the islanders had had enough; after a national campaign and much fundraising, the islanders themselves secured ownership the following year. Now every June, Eigg celebrates its Independence Day in the community hall with a cracking community ceilidh – a raucous live music event that draws plenty of visitors too.

Rum

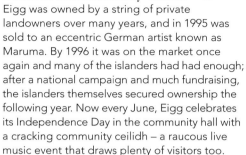

The largest of the Small Isles, Rum is magnificently wild and rugged, dominated by the jagged mountains of its Cuillin ridge. For a long time it was known as 'the forbidden isle', as visitors to the island were discouraged by its private owners, and even after it was sold to the Nature Conservancy Council in 1957 (now Scottish Natural Heritage) it was used as a nature reserve for scientific study. Only in recent years has the area around Kinloch become owned by its local community trust and visiting the island become much easier.

The island is served by CalMac's Small Isles ferry from Mallaig on a complex timetable that takes in a different combination of islands in a different order each day; often the ferry calls at Rum, sails on to Canna and then returns to Rum on the way back to Mallaig, enabling very short day visits for those who don't want to stay over. Only residents are allowed to bring vehicles on the ferry. During the summer months there is also a passenger service on the *M.V. Sheerwater* from Arisaig. The island has a hostel, a bed and breakfast, camping pods and a campsite at Kinloch (pack midge repellent). There are also a couple of remote bothies.

1 Eigg, Rum from the Singing Sands　**2 Eigg,** Kildonan beach　**3 Eigg,** summit of the Sgùrr
4 Eigg, Kildonan Cross　**5 Eigg,** Bay of Laig from near the Finger of God

Visit Kinloch Castle

This massive sandstone edifice was built as a holiday home and shooting lodge by the island's then owners, the Bulloughs – industrialists from Accrington in Lancashire – between 1897 and 1900, and it looks strikingly incongruous in such a place. Today the castle is in a state of decay, but an association has been set up to attempt to safeguard and restore it for the future. It can be visited on a guided tour that usually operates between the times that the ferry calls. The interior is simply astonishing: a bizarre time-capsule of Edwardian opulence and excess, including an automated barrel organ known as an orchestrion and showers that shoot jets of water in all directions.

Watch for otters

A much more recent and fitting construction on the island is the otter hide overlooking Kinloch Bay. Reached by heading up the track from the ferry jetty and then taking a signed path on the left, a lovely ten-minute walk soon leads into woods past some old ruins to reach the hide. Otters are elusive creatures and tend to put in an appearance when least expected – sometimes they can be seen playing around the ferry as it turns in the bay, but they are shy and the hide at least gives you a chance to watch for them undetected. A much rougher walk continues on an often indistinct and boggy path parallel to the coast to reach the atmospheric deserted settlement of Port na Caranean, abandoned when the residents were moved to Kinloch.

1 Rum, Kinloch Castle   **2** Rum, otter hide   **3** Rum, cycling back to Kinloch   **4** Rum, Kilmory Bay with Skye beyond
5 Rum, the deserted village of Port na Caranean   **6** Rum, Harris mausoleum

Hike to the Harris mausoleum

If Kinloch Castle didn't convince you of the size of the Bulloughs' egos, this remarkable building on the wild west coast of the island certainly will. Constructed around 1900 in the form of an enormous Doric temple, it replaced an earlier structure decorated with mosaics that was demolished after someone remarked that it resembled the lavatories at Waterloo station. It has a stunning position above Harris Bay and is linked to Kinloch by eleven kilometres of Land Rover track through the heart of Rum, making for either a very long out-and-back walk, or a ride on a mountain bike (hire is available).

See the deer at Kilmory Bay

Rum is not commonly associated with sandy beaches, but the magnificent sands on the north coast at Kilmory are the exception; they have superb views out to the Cuillin of Skye. The beach is roughly a nine-kilometre hike or bike along a good track from Kinloch, perfect for a bike ride if you don't mind the initial climb. The area behind the beach has been the subject of a continuous study of red deer since 1972, one of the longest running surveys of wild animals in the world. The rut here was featured on BBC TV's *Autumnwatch* series, and you are very likely to see these magnificent creatures as you head to the beach.

Stay in an island bothy

Volunteers from the Mountain Bothies Association maintain around a hundred simple shelters – mostly in old cottages – around Scotland, which offer something like camping but with a roof. They are free to stay in for anyone who follows the bothy code – taking all your litter away and behaving responsibly. Two of the eight bothies situated on islands are on Rum – Dibidil on the rugged southern coastline below the Cuillin, and Guirdil in the remote north-west. Both require challenging hikes to reach, but for those who are properly prepared and equipped they offer an island bothy experience to remember.

Experience the Rum Cuillin

The dark volcanic peaks of the Rum Cuillin dominate the island. Steep, rocky, rugged and challenging, the range is a smaller version of its most famous namesake on the nearby Isle of Skye and offers unmatched views of mountain and sea. The complete traverse – from Kinloch,

over all the peaks and descending to Dibidil bothy – is an epic expedition with tricky terrain and a good deal of scrambling, and is one of the great challenges for UK hill baggers. For the average hillwalker an ascent of Hallival is a dramatic objective from Kinloch in its own right, with only minimal scrambling.

Hear or see the shearwaters

Amazingly, a third of the world's population of Manx shearwaters nest on the Rum Cuillin every summer. You may hear their eerie call from underground on the ridge of Hallival; Norse settlers thought it was the noise of trolls, hence the name of one of the other summits on the ridge, Trollaval. Witnessing 100,000 pairs of birds returning to their burrows to feed their chicks at night is an incredible experience – but remember that these mountains are a challenging enough place even during the daytime, so it's not one open to everyone.

Canna

Canna's position – remote and hidden away behind Rum in views from the mainland coast – has led to it being far less well known than its neighbours. Make no mistake though, this is a beautiful island, with emerald-green pastures, pockets of woodland, wild moors and dramatic cliffs. Canna is owned by the National Trust for Scotland.

Like its Small Isles neighbours, Canna is served by CalMac ferries from Mallaig on a complex timetable that takes in a different combination of islands in a different order each day. The island has a guest house, a small bunkhouse and a campsite including camping pods. There's also a cafe and a small community shop.

See Coroghan Castle

This crumbling ruin is situated atop a dramatic coastal outcrop high above a lovely beach, making it Canna's most picturesque sight. The small rectangular tower is thought to date from the seventeenth century, and according to local tradition it was used as a prison, once employed by Donald Macdonald of Clanranald to confine his wife Marion. It was described by the early traveller Thomas Pennant in 1772 as 'A lofty slender rock, that juts into the sea: on one side is a little tower, at a vast height above us, accessible by a narrow and horrible path: it seems so small as scarce to be able to contain half a dozen people'. Today it is in a dangerous state and is far better appreciated from the sands below.

Get deflected to Compass Hill

North from the foot of Coroghan Castle's crag rises Compass Hill – so named as the magnetic rock of the hill is said to affect the compass needles on passing ships. The ascent of Compass Hill is best made by heading up the landward side of a fence from near Coroghan and passing through a gate. The coastal cliffs become increasingly impressive towards the top of the hill; for a tough and pathless but superb all-day excursion you can make a traverse from here right around Canna's northern coastline.

Discover Gaelic heritage at Canna House

Canna's grandest house was the home of the renowned Gaelic scholar Dr John Lorne Campbell and his wife Margaret Fay Shaw. They dedicated their lives to recording the traditions, folklore and heritage of Hebridean culture, and bequeathed both the house and the whole island to the National Trust for Scotland. The house still contains the remarkable archive they amassed. It's currently closed to the public, but the gardens – entered via a tunnel of escallonia – are worth the visit.

1 Canna, view to Rum from souterrains **2** Rum, on Hallival, looking to Askival **3** Canna, coast near Compass Hill **4** Canna, cafe **5** Canna, Coroghan Castle

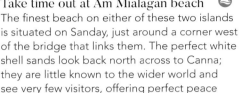

1 Sanday, Am Mialagan beach   **2 Sanday,** Dun Mor

Go underground at the souterrains

There's a wealth of more ancient remains to be found around the island, including an early Christian cross and a prominent standing stone amongst the bluebells, both situated fairly near the shop and cafe. A much longer walk is needed to visit the souterrains – reached by following the main track as far as Tarbet Bay until a marker indicates the start of a faint, boggy path heading north. These underground passages date from prehistoric times and are thought to have been used to store food. With care you can lower yourself into the entrance to feel how much cooler they are inside; the large stones lining the sides and roof of the passageway can still be seen.

Eat truly local at Cafe Canna

This tiny whitewashed cafe has an enviable location on the sheltered southern shoreline looking across to neighbouring Sanday. Don't be deceived by its modest appearance, the menu here includes truly local food such as Canna rabbit stew, lobster landed here on the island, Arisaig moules frites and haddock in Skye Ale batter; bookings are highly recommended for evening meals.
www.cafecanna.co.uk

Sanday

Connected to Canna at low tide by mudflats and sand – and at high tide by a bridge – Sanday provides shelter to the pier that serves the two islands. There's a string of buildings along the north shore facing its larger neighbour with which it really forms a single community. The impressive deconsecrated St Edward's Church once operated as a hostel and Gaelic study centre but is now locked, and there's a self-catering cottage for rent but no other facilities for visitors to the island.

Take time out at Am Mialagan beach

The finest beach on either of these two islands is situated on Sanday, just around a corner west of the bridge that links them. The perfect white shell sands look back north across to Canna; they are little known to the wider world and see very few visitors, offering perfect peace and solitude.

Peek at the puffins on the stack of Dun Mor

The great blocky sea stack of Dun Mor stands detached from the dramatic cliffs of Sanday's south-eastern corner and presents the island's finest scenic feature. It's a fair yomp over some pathless moorland to see the stack, which is worth it for the rock scenery alone. However, in early summer there's another compelling reason to make the effort, as the stack is the home to a large colony of puffins, filling the air above it when seen from the nearby clifftop. Great skuas are well aware of the puffins too and these airborne pirates can often be seen harrying the puffins as they bring in their beakfuls of sand eels.

Muck

The smallest of the Small Isles, Muck appears from a distance to be relatively low-lying and lacking in the distinctive features that make its neighbours so enticing. Appearances are deceptive, however, as Muck is a wee gem. Most of the island consists of a single farm at Gallanach, while many of the small population of thirty-eight live in and around Port Mor where the ferry calls.

Muck is served by CalMac's Small Isles ferry service from Mallaig on four or five days each week, based on a complex timetable that takes in a different combination of islands in a different order each day. There's a surprising amount of accommodation available, with a fine modern country lodge, several self-catering cottages, a bed and breakfast, a bunkhouse and a yurt. There's also a craft shop and cafe.

Cross Muck to Gallanach Bay

The only road on the island runs from the ferry jetty at Port Mor in the south to Gallanach on the north coast, where the fine sands look north towards Rum. If you aren't wanting just to sit on the beach, you can walk further, passing the farm buildings and heading on to the Aird nan Uan peninsula, which gives rougher walking. Near the end is a ring of stones – the remains of a Bronze Age cairn and more recent graves. Beyond it is Eilean Aird nan Uan, or Lamb Island. Not really an island at all, it can be reached by a wee scramble except at the highest tide. Further out is Eilean nan Each – Horse Island – which is linked to Muck by seaweed-covered rocks only briefly at the lowest spring tides.

Climb Beinn Airein

The trig point marking the summit of Beinn Airein may be only 138 metres above the sea, but its dramatic position and 360-degree panorama make the ascent well worth the effort. Begin the climb from Gallanach, passing to the right of the farm buildings and then turning left through a small gate, following tractor tracks uphill initially; there's no path up the hill but there are gates as you make the climb.

Indulge yourself at the Muck tea room

It may look like a simple stone bothy, but Muck's tea room is an unmissable port of call on any visit to the island. Just about everything is home-made, including all the cakes, soup and bread, but perhaps best of all are the huge set-menu evening meals, which must be booked in advance. It's a craft shop too, specialising in hand-knitted clothing and homespun wool. *www.isleofmuck.com*

Stay in a yurt

Though there are other islands with yurts – including neighbouring Eigg – few can match the experience of a stay in Muck's solitary yurt. Set on the west coast, the sunsets from here – looking out to the mountains of Rum – are simply unforgettable. The yurt houses a stove and has both a double bed and additional camp beds, and a gas hob and grill, though you'll have to pop outside to use the composting loo.

Eilean Shona

Shona guards the entrance to Loch Moidart. between the Moidart and Ardnamurchan peninsulas of the mainland. Its eastern half is richly wooded, while to the west it rises to rugged, bare hills and a height of 265 metres at Beinn a' Bhaillidh. The eastern part of the island is accessible at low tide via a tidal causeway and track from the A861 road, but its main house and cottages are usually reached via a boat to a pier that looks out to Castle Tioram in Moidart. There is no regular boat service for visitors, but most of the cottages and the house itself are available for short-term holiday rentals – guests are picked up on a RIB.

1 Muck, Gallanach Bay and Eigg **2** Muck, yurt **3** Muck, tea room **4** Muck, graves at Aird nan Uan

The Isle of Skye is world renowned for its stunning landscapes, from the Alp-like peaks of the Cuillin to the remarkable landslips of the Trotternish peninsula, and from its fascinating history to its complex and spectacular coastline. Although it's the most visited of all the islands in this book, Skye is a big place and it's worth taking the time to explore far from the beaten track and discover its hidden gems. It is surrounded by many smaller islands, of which Raasay is the largest, with a character all its own and offering an easy escape from its better-known neighbour.

North of Skye there are groups of tiny islands close to the west coast and continuing around the north coast. The Summer Isles near Ullapool are perhaps the best known of these, but – further north still – Handa offers the perfect island day trip.

SKYE & THE NORTH-WEST

Opposite Skye, Neist Point **Overleaf** Skye, Quiraing

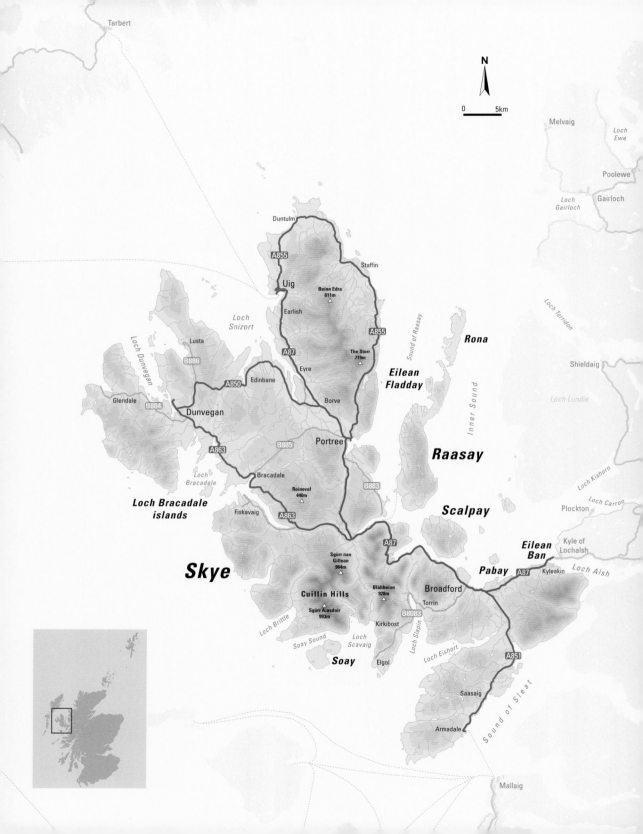

Skye

The best known of all Scottish islands, Skye occupies an almost mythical place in the minds of many. Its Gaelic name *An t-Eilean Sgitheanach* – 'the Winged Isle' – refers to its complex shape with many projecting peninsulas. The island has some of our most dramatic landscapes, from the jagged Cuillin mountains and the landslips of the Trotternish Ridge to some superb coastal cliffs. This physical drama combines with the island's rich history to create a truly special place.

The graceful arch of the Skye Bridge has connected the island to Kyle of Lochalsh on the mainland since 1995; it is free to cross. There's also a regular CalMac vehicle ferry from Mallaig that lands at Armadale on the Sleat peninsula. In the north the port of Uig has ferry services that connect Skye to North Uist and Harris in the Outer Hebrides. The island has a wide range of facilities and services, with its main centres of population being the picturesque capital at Portree and the straggling village of Broadford.

Watch the sunset from Neist Point

Skye's most westerly headland is home to one of the most dramatically situated lighthouses in Scotland. Driving there can be an adventure in itself, as this is the furthest part of the island from the bridge, and the last few kilometres are on a narrow and twisting single-track road. You can visit the lighthouse by a moderate walk, heading down concrete steps and bypassing the fine cliffs of An t-Aigeach – 'the Stallion'. The best views, however, are just north along the cliff edge from the tiny parking area; the views from here out to the Point and North Uist beyond are breathtaking – especially at sunset.

Pay your respects to the Old Man

This fifty-metre-tall pinnacle of basalt stands at the foot of the great cliffs of the Storr, and together with them is an iconic landmark. The Old Man is well seen from across the waters of Loch Fada when driving north from Portree, but for a close-up visit there's a parking area at the start of a well-maintained path that leads up towards its base. Reaching the pinnacle is a stiff climb but well worth it to explore the Sanctuary – the remarkable amphitheatre of rock scenery that the Old Man guards.

Taste a dram of Talisker

Talisker distillery at Carbost on the shores of Loch Harport has been producing whisky since 1830. The distillery tours – available throughout the year – conclude with a tasting of this sweet and smoky, peaty single malt that seems to absorb the flavour of its maritime setting. After you've visited the distillery – and if you have a driver – it's well worth taking a trip to nearby Talisker beach, nestled between high cliffs, where the black and white sands mingle into beautiful patterns.

Visit the cleared village of Boreraig

Skye is full of romantic connections with the story of Bonnie Prince Charlie's escape from his pursuers in the aftermath of the Jacobite defeat at Culloden, as celebrated in the Skye Boat Song. But there's a darker history here too, as the Highland Clearances saw many Skye folk driven from their land to make way for sheep farms. The landscape is dotted with deserted former settlements, and none are more atmospheric than the ruins of Boreraig on the north shore of Loch Eishort. This haunting place is reached by a path over the hills from the ruined church of Cill Chriosd on the Elgol road; it's possible to continue along the coast to Suisnish and Camas Malag to make a memorable day's walking.

1 Skye, cleared village of Boreraig   **2 Skye**, view over the Cuillin from Bla Bheinn
3 Skye, coral beach at Claigan   **4 Skye**, Loch Coruisk   **5 Skye**, Talisker Bay

Marvel at the Quiraing

This fantastical rock landscape must be one of the strangest in Scotland. Formed by a series of enormous landslips, this northern part of the Trotternish Ridge has remarkable features such as the Table – a flat, grassy platform surrounded by craggy cliffs, the Needle – a great pinnacle of rock, and the craggy fortress of the Prison. A spectacular and narrow mountain road winds up to cross the ridge just south of the Quiraing and brings this amazing place within easy reach. A rocky path – with scrambling at one point – leads north from the top of the road and passes beneath the cliffs to reach the heart of the Quiraing.

Take a boat trip to Loch Coruisk

Loch Coruisk lies at the heart of the Cuillin, Britain's most alpine mountain range. The waters of this remote and remarkable place can be reached by a long and difficult walk, but it's easier and perhaps more enjoyable to take one of the regular boat trips from Elgol. The boat crosses the seas of Loch Scavaig to reach a landing stage from which it's just a short walk away. Surrounded by gaunt peaks of bare rock, the loch featured on the Grand Tour in the Victorian era and was celebrated in verse by Sir Walter Scott and Alfred Lord Tennyson, as well as being painted by J.M.W. Turner.

Conquer a Cuillin

The Cuillin mountains dominate the famed views from Sligachan and Elgol, and just a glance at them reveals that any ascents here are generally much more serious undertakings than hillwalks on the mainland. Bruach na Frithe and Sgurr na Banachdaich are perhaps the most accessible peaks for skilled and experienced mountain walkers, but even these require great care and skilled route finding. Reaching any one of the major Cuillin summits is, however, an unforgettable experience; there are a good number of mountain guides available on the island who can help you realise your mountaineering dreams.

Climb Ben Tianavaig

A more modest objective for the humble hillwalker is this fine miniature mountain that dominates the coastline south of Portree. The half-day ascent from the pretty bay at Camustianavaig deserves to be regarded as a classic – a climb along a magnificent escarpment which rises high above the sea. The summit view is quite unforgettable, in particular looking back down the escarpment to the Cuillin and the Red Hills. There's also an aerial view of Portree to the north backed by all the drama of Trotternish, while Raasay closes the horizon to the east.

Chill on the coral beaches

While Skye is an island of superlatives, its fame doesn't rest on its sandy beaches. Talisker, Staffin, Camas Daraich and An Aird in the Braes are all worth a visit, but it's the 'coral' beaches near Claigan that are deservedly the best known. Accessed by an easy two-kilometre walk, a close look at the white sands here reveals them to be made of maerl, a dried and calcified seaweed. And for the dedicated island bagger there's a bonus in that the minor tidal island of Lampay is only just offshore.

Dine at the Three Chimneys

When Shirley Spear and her husband Eddie first realised their ambition to open a bistro-style eatery on Skye back in 1985, few would have guessed that the restaurant would develop into the culinary institution it has become today. Often featured in lists of the world's finest restaurants, the Three Chimneys still operates in the same humble whitewashed croft house, with stone walls and wooden beams within. This is fine dining with prices to match, but the

1 Skye, throwing the hammer at the Skye Games   **2 Skye**, pipe bands at the Skye Games   **3 Skye**, the Quiraing from Staffin
4 Skye, Rubha Hunish   **5 Skye**, Sgurr na h-Uamha in the Cuillin   **6 Skye**, Museum of Island Life

restaurant really makes the most of the island's superb fresh ingredients and this is an excellent Skye, land and sea foodie experience.
www.threechimneys.co.uk

Tackle the Skye Trail

For backpackers who enjoy a real challenge, hiking the 128-kilometre Skye Trail makes for an unforgettable experience. It's unofficial and still unmarked, but for those with the necessary experience and navigation skills it's the perfect way to enjoy Skye in a week. The trail includes a traverse of the Trotternish Ridge, has some remarkable coastal sections, and passes through the shadow of the dramatic Cuillin, before reaching journey's end in Broadford. Whether you prefer to make use of island hospitality or opt for the freedom of a tent, the Skye Trail is a fitting match for the island's epic landscapes.
www.skyetrail.org.uk

Soak up the atmosphere at Dun Scaith

The woodlands of the Sleat peninsula have led to it being known as 'the Garden of Skye', but taking the twisting and challenging minor loop road through Ord and Tokavaig offers an entirely different experience. The gem of this undiscovered corner of the island is the dramatic ruin of Dun Scaith castle on the shores of Loch Eishort. Set on a rocky promontory high above the sea, this thirteenth-century castle was once accessed via a high drawbridge. Now ruined, it's an atmospheric spot with an unforgettable view, and was heavily featured in Macpherson's mythic Ossian poems.

Watch for whales at Rubha Hunish

A former coastguard station – now a bothy open to all – is perched atop dramatic columnar basalt cliffs that overlook Skye's most northerly promontory, Rubha Hunish. An ingenious old

path makes the awkward descent to this furthest headland, and walkers who make the effort are rewarded with superb rock scenery including stacks and geos. In the summer months the furthest point is one of the best places in Britain for watching cetaceans; minke whales visit frequently as the currents around the headland lead to plentiful supplies of food.

Museum of Island Life

Skye has a number of museums but this collection of seven traditional thatched cottages at Kilmuir stands out. It was begun by a local man back in 1965, then containing only the Old Croft House which was lived in until only a few years previously. The peat fire is always lit, and together with the other cottages the museum gives an impression of life on the island at the close of the nineteenth century. One of the cottages contains an archive of photographs and documents recording much local history, and near the entrance to the museum is the impressive grave of Flora MacDonald, who helped Bonnie Prince Charlie to escape to the island as remembered in the Skye Boat Song.
www.skyemuseum.co.uk

Go to the Skye Games

Attending a Highland Games is a quintessential Scottish experience, and the Skye Games – held in Portree each year since 1877 – are one of the largest in the islands, always making for a fabulous day out. The grassy amphitheatre of An Meall (unromantically translated as 'the Lump') provides a perfect venue for the traditional mix of 'heavy' events (hammer throwing, caber-tossing), track and field, a hill race, highland dancing, piping and tug o' war. The massed pipe bands are a real spectacle, and the Portree games also adds sailing and rowing events to the usual mix.

Loch Bracadale islands

There are four main islands in Loch Bracadale – Wiay (the largest), Harlosh and Tarner islands, and Oronsay. All have fine cliff features and enjoy superlative views towards the Cuillin, but none have a boat service – or any people living on them. Oronsay is, however, accessible from Skye at low tide via a natural stony causeway, enabling walkers to make a memorable visit with careful observation of the tide times.

Take a hike to Oronsay

The five-kilometre out-and-back walk begins from the end of a minor road near Ullinish, following a grass track over some boggy ground to reach the causeway that leads across to the island. This causeway is submerged for around two hours either side of high tide, so keep an eye on the time to ensure you don't become stranded. Once on the island the clifftops make for a grand short walk; they rise to seventy-four metres towards the south-west end – the highest point of the Bracadale islands – and the views are superb.

Soay

At over 1,000 hectares Soay is almost as large as nearby Canna, but its position off Skye's coast beneath the great mountains of the Cuillin leaves it feeling dwarfed. In 1851 the population here peaked at a remarkable 158 people, many of them fleeing clearances on its larger neighbour. After the Second World War the island was bought by the eccentric aristocrat Gavin Maxwell, who later found fame as the author of *Ring of Bright Water*, an account of his life with otters on the Glenelg peninsula. He used the island as the base for a commercial basking shark fishery, but the business soon floundered; by 1952 most of the islanders petitioned the government for evacuation to Mull. There are currently two or three permanent inhabitants but there are no regular boats for visitors. It is possible to charter a boat trip from Elgol, and during the summer there's a weekly non-landing cruise from Kinloch on Rum.

1 Oronsay, on the clifftops   **2** Oronsay causeway, from Skye
3 Eilean Ban, Gavin Maxwell's house   **4** Eilean Ban and the Skye Bridge

Eilean Ban

The best known of several small islands set off the coast around the Kyle of Lochalsh, Eilean Ban – or the White Island – is briefly visited by thousands of people every day as the Skye Bridge road leads across it. There's more to the island than most of them suspect, however, as the island has a fine lighthouse and was the last home of the author Gavin Maxwell.

Visit the last home of Gavin Maxwell

The best way to start your adventure to Eilean Ban is at the Bright Water Centre in nearby Kyleakin. The island was purchased by Gavin Maxwell late in his life, and after his retreat at Sandaig was destroyed by fire, he moved to Eilean Ban and lived his final years here. The living room of the cottages – which Maxwell made into one long room – is now a museum to the incredible life of this great eccentric. Tours of the island can be booked at the centre and include a visit that provides an insight into the life of this complex man. If you are exceptionally lucky you might catch a glimpse of an otter.

Pabay

This low-lying island is well seen from Broadford Bay; its 122 hectares are still worked as a single farm. The island is perhaps best known amongst philatelists as special stamps are issued to convey post from the island to the mainland – and are sought after by collectors. There's a fine shell beach to the northern shores, but there is no regular boat access for visitors.

Scalpay

Scalpay dominates the view for several kilometres when driving north along Skye's main road from Broadford, an aspect that emphasises its bleak and rugged character. It rises to a height of 396 metres at Mullach na Carn, a fine viewpoint. Today the island is home to a single family, and there are three holiday cottages available for rent. Aside from those who have booked one of the cottages there are no regular boat trips.

Raasay

The largest of the satellite islands off the coastline of Skye, Raasay is a real gem – especially when its busier, more glamorous neighbour is teeming with visitors. Almost twenty kilometres long and three to four kilometres wide, its landscape is dominated by the flat-topped volcanic summit of Dun Caan.

The island is served by a regular CalMac vehicle ferry from Sconser on Skye. There is a well-stocked community shop in its main settlement, Inverarish, and accommodation options include several bed and breakfasts, more upmarket rooms at the distillery and Raasay House, and self-catering cottages.

Climb Dun Caan

Reaching Raasay's highest summit (444 metres) has long been an objective of visitors to the island. As part of his famed tour of the Highlands and Islands with Dr Samuel Johnson, James Boswell made the ascent and was so delighted with the view that he danced a jig upon the summit. The ascent is a moderate hillwalk; there is a rough path from the old ironstone mine on the road above Inverarish, close enough to the ferry pier to make bringing a vehicle unnecessary. If you get a clear day you'll share Boswell's joy at the 360-degree vista of sea and mountains.

Feel the past at Hallaig

The most celebrated son of Raasay was the great Gaelic poet Sorley MacLean, whose work is at the heart of the language's cultural renaissance. One of his most renowned works, *Hallaig*, is a symbolic poem inspired by the ruins and history of the cleared village of the same name, set above Raasay's eastern coastline.

A path from the end of the North Fearns road leads to a monument a short distance short of the site of the village; it is inscribed with the words of the poem in both Gaelic and MacLean's own English translation. The ruins themselves can be reached by continuing on from the monument, passing through the birch wood mentioned in the poem – though the going underfoot becomes rougher.

Take Calum's Road

For many years Raasay's slender ribbon of tarmac road ended near Brochel Castle, some two and a half kilometres short of the community at Arnish in the north. The inhabitants campaigned unsuccessfully over several decades for the council to provide a road, but to no avail, and the population at Arnish dwindled. One man decided to take matters into his own hands. Calum MacLeod, a local crofter and the assistant keeper of the lighthouse on Rona, had learned road-making from a book and began work himself in 1964, with a shovel, pick-axe and wheelbarrow. It took him ten years to complete the road, after which it was finally adopted and surfaced by the council, though by then Calum and his wife were the last inhabitants of Arnish. You can drive the road, park at Brochel and walk it, or, perhaps best of all, bike it in a grand ride from the ferry. If undertaking the latter you will appreciate that Calum's Road is better graded than the rest of Raasay's road network.

Raasay distillery

After learning about the struggles of Raasay's difficult past, it's good to be able to raise a dram to the island's future. You can do so at the end of a tour of its state-of-the-art distillery. Using barley grown in adjacent fields, dried using local peat, and water that has flowed

1 **Raasay**, North Fearns   2 and 3 **Raasay**, distillery **Photos:** Isle of Raasay Distillery
4 **Raasay**, Calum's Road   5 **Raasay**, Dun Caan

down through the island's volcanic rocks, this new distillery is maturing all its spirit on site. The aim is to make a lightly peated dram which will be matured in three different kinds of oak casks. The first single malt will be available in 2020, and before then you can enjoy a dram of 'Raasay While We Wait' – a dram created to give an impression of the kind of whisky the distillers are aiming for.

www.raasaydistillery.com

Eilean Fladday

This tidal island is separated from Raasay by the narrows of Caol Fladda, a couple of kilometres north from Arnish. The path to it was built by Calum MacLeod and his brother Charles under a contract with the council between 1949 and 1952, and it was here that Calum perfected the road-building skills which later earned him his fame. The island had five families in the 1920s, but the last left in 1965; today the remaining cottages are only used for part of the year. Walkers can cross to the island at low tide, but care is needed to avoid becoming stranded.

Rona

Not to be confused with North Rona, isolated far from Lewis, this Rona is set to the immediate north of Raasay. Its landscape of bare Lewisian gneiss – one of the oldest rocks in Europe – is punctuated by small pockets of natural woodland. There is no regular boat access for visitors except those who have booked in one of the three holiday cottages here. An Acarsaid Mhor provides a picturesque natural harbour and an approach for kayakers.

Isle of Ewe

Some three and a half kilometres long and around one kilometre wide, the Isle of Ewe takes up a surprisingly extensive part of Loch Ewe. It was once home to several families, but is now uninhabited, and the loch itself was used as a naval anchorage during the Second World War. There is no regular access, but it may be possible to arrange a boat from nearby Aultbea.

Gruinard Island

Set offshore from one of the Highlands' most picturesque beaches, the recent history of Gruinard Island is a dark one. The island has been uninhabited since the 1920s, but in 1942 it became the site of an experiment in biological warfare. The ground was deliberately contaminated with anthrax bombs so as to infect the sheep which were used in the experiment, and the final report concluded that anthrax could be used to make cities uninhabitable for 'generations'. The island was left in this state until 1981 when a group calling itself Operation Dark Harvest wrote to newspapers threatening to leave soil samples from the island at 'appropriate points' to raise public awareness and demanding a clean-up. Two packets were left at government locations, and in 1986 a project began to decontaminate Gruinard. In 1990 it was declared clean, but many have publicly doubted whether this is the case. It's probably not at the top of many people's intended island bagging lists!

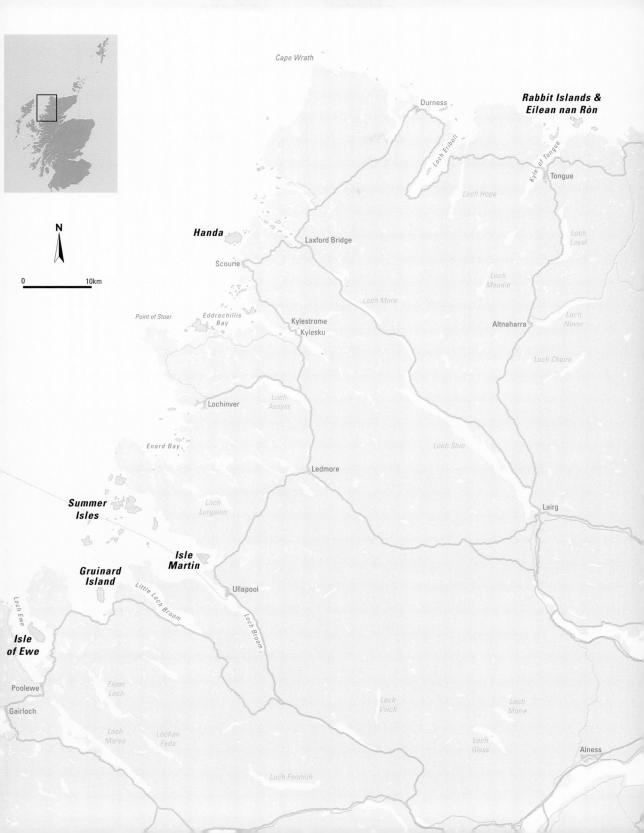

Summer Isles

This extensive archipelago of smaller islands is scattered in the outermost reaches of Loch Broom. Stretching from Priest Island in the south-west to Horse Island in the east and Isle Ristol and Eilean Mullagrach in the north, there are around twenty isles and islets in the group, although only Tanera Mor is inhabited. In the summer season boat trips are available from Ullapool and Achiltibuie; these include both cruises around the islands. The name 'Summerisle' was used as the island home of a pagan sect in the cult film *The Wicker Man*, though the film itself was shot in Galloway and at Plockton.

Cruise around Tanera Mor

Tanera Mor was one of the settings described by the ecologist Frank Fraser Darling in his fascinating book *Island Years*, published in 1940. Together with his wife and young son, he set up a home on the island in 1939 and tried to reclaim the derelict land for agricultural production. Subsequently he became one of Britain's most prominent voices in the ecology movement, and an expert on both the human and natural economy of the Highlands.

For many years the island was perhaps best known for the special stamps, sold at its tiny cafe and shop, which were issued to carry mail to the mainland (you still needed to affix a Royal Mail stamp to ensure onwards delivery). The island was placed on the market in 2013 and

1 Eilean Fladday, causeway from Raasay   **2 Isle of Ewe,** from near Aultbea   **3 Tanera Beag,** the Cathedral Cave
4 Tanera Mor, with the CalMac ferry to Stornoway, and Stac Pollaidh beyond

briefly lost its resident family; however, a new owner began a major development in 2017 to make the island 'an idyllic retreat' for guests. At the time of writing it is unclear whether regular landing trips will operate in the future and whether the island stamps will be on sale.

Enter the Cathedral Cave on Tanera Beag

Tanera Beag is an uninhabited island set a kilometre west of its larger neighbour and sometimes used for grazing sheep. It is best known for a fine sea cave – Cathedral Cave, or *An Eaglais Mhor* in the original Gaelic – in its south-western cliffs. This is often visited by keen kayakers as well as the boat trips which, if the weather permits, take visitors right into its spectacular opening.

Isle Martin

South-east of the Summer Isles, Isle Martin was the site of an early monastery, and its more fertile southern part was used for crofting until the 1960s. A new owner then began establishing the island as a nature reserve and gifted it to the RSPB in 1980 to be managed for conservation. Its location made it a difficult property and the charity gifted the island to a community trust run by locals on the nearby mainland. It is possible to visit the island as a volunteer for the Isle Martin Trust in July and August, or to rent one of the old houses. There are plans to develop the facilities which will begin with improvements to the pontoon.

Handa

Set off the coast of Sutherland near Scourie, Handa is a gem. It lost its indigenous population following the potato famine in 1847, and today it's a nature reserve in the care of the Scottish Wildlife Trust, renowned for its seabirds. Its landscape has remarkable variety for its size, from a perfect sandy beach in the south to dramatic cliffs around its northern coastline.

There's a regular passenger ferry service that runs through the summer season – except on Sundays – from the hamlet of Tarbet.

See the Great Stack

There's a superb marked circular walk around Handa which is simply unmissable. The highlight is the spectacular northern coast, where the Great Stack of Handa stands detached just offshore. The stack is home to a colony of puffins. Handa once had a large population of rats which decimated its birdlife, until the rodents were eradicated by the Wildlife Trust back in 1997, but most puffins still prefer the safety of the stack. Incredibly, the top of the stack was reached back in the nineteenth century by a group of lads from Lewis who traversed across to it hand-over-hand in what is one of the first recorded instances of climbing for sport.

Get dive-bombed by an arctic skua

Every spring a colony of these spectacular birds come to Handa to nest, and if you visit at the right time then getting attacked by them is one island experience you are unlikely to be able to avoid! These pirates of the seas get their food by aggressively harassing other seabirds, and they are not afraid to have a go at human visitors too when they feel you are too close to their nests. The species is actually red-listed and in serious decline, and short of heading to Orkney or Shetland, this is your best chance to see them.

Rabbit Islands and Eilean nan Ròn

There are surprisingly few significant islands off Scotland's northern coastline, west of Orkney. The Rabbit Islands out in Tongue Bay are linked to the mainland at the lowest of tides, and are fringed with sandy beaches. North-east of them is the larger Eilean nan Ròn – the island of the seals, very well-named as around 350 pups are born here each year. The island once supported a human population too, until the last locals were evacuated in 1931. Closer to the mainland is Neave or Coomb Island which once had a monastery dedicated to St Columba but no trace of this now remains. None of these islands have any regular boat access.

1 Handa, ferry landing on the beach   **2** Handa, the Great Stack   **3** Handa, Arctic skua   **4** Handa, clifftop walking

Known to Gaelic-speaking locals as *Na h-Eileanan Siar*, 'the Western Isles', this great island chain is a place apart. Stretching from the Butt of Lewis in the north to Barra and its neighbours in the south, the Outer Hebrides have a character all their own. There's something of everything here, from the great mountains of Harris and North Uist to as fine an array of sandy beaches as you'll find anywhere in the world; from a harsh history of forced clearances to today's culture, rich in music and with the Gaelic language thriving. Many of the larger islands are now connected by causeways, with a few gaps served by inter-island ferries.

THE OUTER HEBRIDES

Opposite North Uist, Phobuil Fhin   **Overleaf** Berneray, West beach

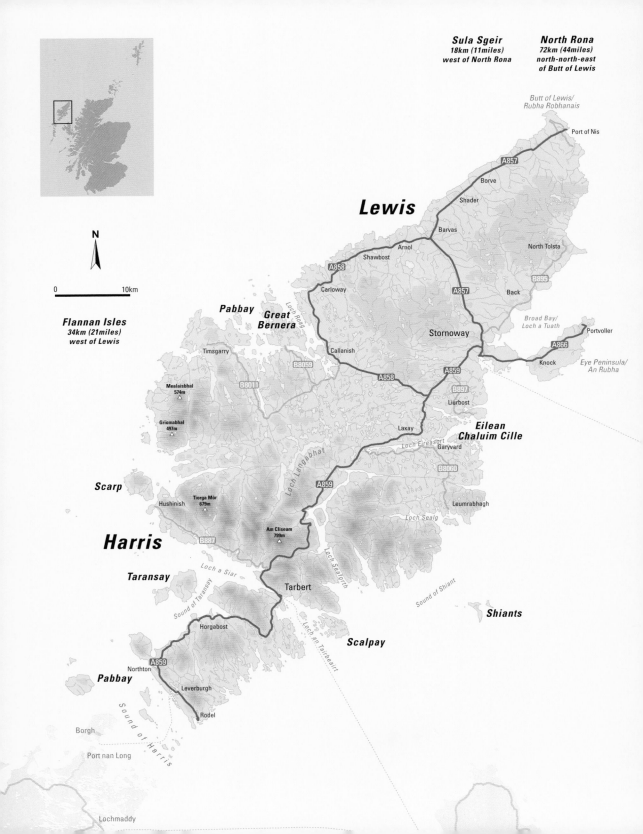

Sula Sgeir
18km (11miles)
west of North Rona

North Rona
72km (44miles)
north-north-east
of Butt of Lewis

Butt of Lewis/
Rubha Robhanais

Port of Nis

A857

Borve

Shader

Lewis

North Tolsta

Barvas

Arnol

Shawbost

A858

Back

B895

Carloway

A857

N

Stornoway

Broad Bay/
Loch a Tuath

Portvoller

0   10km

Pabbay **Great
Bernera**

Callanish

A866

Knock

Eye Peninsula/
An Rubha

Flannan Isles
34km (21miles)
west of Lewis

Timsgarry

B8059

Loch Roag

A858

A859

B897

Liurbost

Mealaisbhal
574m

B8011

**Eilean
Chaluim Cille**

Griomabhal
497m

Laxay

Scarp

Loch Langabhat

Loch Fireasort

Garyvard

B8060

Hushinish

Tiorga Mòr
679m

A859

Loch Sealg

Leumrabhagh

Harris

Am Cliseam
799m

B887

Taransay

Loch a Siar

Loch Seaforth

Loch a Tarbhairt

Tarbert

Sound of Shiant

Shiants

Sound of Taransay

Scalpay

Horgabost

A859

Loch an Tairbeairt

Northton

Pabbay

Leverburgh

Rodel

Borgh

S o u n d   o f   H a r r i s

Port nan Long

Lochmaddy

Lewis

The most intriguing thing about the Isle of Lewis (Eilean Leodhais) is that it isn't an individual island at all. Its conjoined twin, the Isle of Harris, comprises the southernmost third of the land mass, divided by rocky mountains from Lewis in the north. Lewis has the largest population in the Hebrides and contains the administrative capital of the Western Isles (or Outer Hebrides), Stornoway.

The main ferry route to Lewis plies between Ullapool and Stornoway. Taking just under three hours, the service runs twice a day, with extra sailings during peak summer times and reducing to one sailing on winter Sundays. There is also the option of taking the ferry from Uig on Skye to Tarbet in Harris and continuing by car, bus or bicycle on to Lewis. Ferry operator CalMac also sells a Hopscotch ticket which allows numerous combined journeys within the Outer Hebrides on one ticket. All of these ferries take vehicles. Air travel has increased in recent years with regular direct flights to Stornoway from Glasgow, Inverness, Edinburgh and Manchester. Loganair is the main operator.

Lewis has all major services and a good mix of accommodation options. However, as most of the settlements are on the coast with major services centred in and around Stornoway, do bear in mind that in remote places the nearest shop or petrol station can be a long way away. Note that most services are closed on Sundays, including the big supermarket in Stornoway, so you may need to plan ahead. However things are changing fast and it's no longer the case that tourists go hungry on the sabbath as many more cafes, hotels and restaurants open their doors.

See the Butt

Keep heading north and you will eventually reach the most northerly point on the island, the Butt of Lewis. Topped by an unusual brick-built lighthouse, this spot gained a place in the *Guinness Book of Records* for being the windiest place in the UK. It's certainly always pretty breezy, but on stormy days the waves crashing against the high cliffs and sea stacks become truly spectacular. If the elements allow, a dramatic circular walk leads along the coast to the stunning sands of nearby Eoropie beach, passing a natural arch on the way. Behind the dunes lies one of the largest and best equipped play parks in Scotland – be warned it can be hard to prise children of all ages away.

Take the peat road

The Pentland road (Rathad a' Phentland) stretches across the wild open moors between Stornoway and Carloway in the west. Originally planned as a railway which it was hoped would hasten the transport of fish from the fishing station at Carloway on towards markets on the mainland, the road was completed in 1921. Driving, cycling or running across this seemingly desolate landscape reveals a land carved by local hands for generations. The deep peat cuttings on both sides of the road, many of which are still worked today, are the scars where peat has been hefted from the sodden ground. This was traditionally a communal effort, with peats being cut in late spring and left to dry on the ground for a month or so before being piled on to carefully constructed stacks usually adjacent to the house and in past times often rivalling the size of the house itself. Peat burns fairly cool so a household could easily get through 1,500 peats in a winter. Nowadays, less backbreaking forms of heating are available,

131

but many locals still have the rights to cut peats from a personally allocated peat bank, and sales of the tairsgear, a traditional peat cutting tool, have risen recently as more people use this free, if labour-intensive, form of fuel. While the peat road is used as a shortcut by some locals, it can feel utterly deserted and desolate – especially with a storm brewing. A good place to recall stories of ancient bog burials, or as the setting for the latest of Peter May's Lewis-based tartan-noir novels, but not a place to break down. The views are best when heading west, but if cycling the headwinds can be cruel and facing east is the better option.

Stand amidst the stones at Callanish

Visit the windswept site at Callanish at sunset or early morning and watch the light change on these enormous prehistoric standing stones. Five rows of stones form a large cross shape, and near the centre of the arrangement stands a massive monolith almost five metres high. The stones are thought to date from between 2900 and 2600 BC, with a later chambered cairn lying in their midst. While some stones line up with various phases of the moon, the true purpose of the site remains unknown, although local folklore explains the stones are the petrified remains of giants who refused to convert to Christianity. There's a visitor centre and several smaller stone circles nearby.

Cross the Bridge to Nowhere

This curious, well-constructed bridge was once part of an ambitious plan by the island's one-time owner, Lord Leverhulme, to build a road up the east coast of Lewis. The bridge lies just north of Tolsta near a spectacular beach, and is all that remains of the grand plans for a road all the way to Ness. The road, now just

a rough track, peters out about a mile further on with the rest of the route a tough walk over relentless bog and dramatic coastal ravines and clifftops. The bridge features in Peter May's thriller *The Chessmen* as the scene of a teenage scooter race.

Leverhulme owned Lewis and Harris between 1918 and 1923. Having made his fortune in soap (the company eventually became the global giant Unilever), the English businessman turned his attention to projects aimed at modernising and industrialising this outpost of the British Isles. Many of his projects proved overly ambitious or lacked much local support; the Bridge to Nowhere provides a monument to folly.

Retreat to Dun Carloway broch

Explore the double-walled tower that would once have provided a defensive refuge for locals during Norse raids. Built in the first century, Dun Carloway is a fine example of a broch, a round and heavily fortified structure unique to Scotland. This impressive ruin sits alongside an underground visitor centre which can be used as the starting point for a rugged moorland and lochans circular walk.

Na Gearrannan blackhouse village and the west side

The best of the west coast scenery is revealed to those who venture on foot. A challenging nineteen-kilometre linear hike from Bragar takes in natural arches, sea stacks and sandy coves and as it mirrors a bus route it's possible to cut this linear walk short at a number of places. The cliffs are perfect for watching seabirds as well as keeping an eye out for passing sea creatures, including dolphins, porpoises, whales and – of course – curious seals. The added

1 **Lewis**, lighthouse at the Butt   2 **Lewis**, peat stack   3 **Lewis**, Callanish stone circle
4 **Lewis**, Dun Carloway broch   5 **Lewis**, Bridge to Nowhere   6 **Lewis**, Na Gearrannan blackhouse village

bonus is that the hike ends at the atmospheric Na Gearrannan blackhouse village, a restored thatched settlement where, in addition to visiting a museum, you can stay overnight as some of the cottages provide self-catering and hostel accommodation.

Enjoy a well-earned strupag

Around half the 27,000 people living in the Outer Hebrides can speak Gaelic and you will encounter the Celtic language everywhere – road signs, menus, place names, songs and in overheard conversations on the bus or in the cafe. While there's no necessity to learn any Gaelic to visit this bilingual outpost, it's fun to pick up a few words to help understand the names on the map and local names for the wildlife. Local ceilidhs will often include Gaelic singing – keep an eye out for Feis events or the annual HebCelt Festival. There are a number of leaflets and websites that can help, but chance encounters with native speakers, maybe over a *strupag* – or cuppa – in your B&B, can be more illuminating. *Slàinte!*

Dig in at Uig sands

These fabulous sands are where the Lewis chessmen were unearthed in 1831 by a local crofter. Carved from walrus ivory in the twelfth century, they are likely to be Norse, this part of Scotland being under Norwegian rule at that time. The pieces are incredibly lifelike, many with expressions we now associate with boredom, madness and grumpiness. Experts believe the ninety-three-piece hoard may actually be made up from five different chess sets, but this is a place to abandon all thought of treasure hunting to instead relax on Lewis's most spectacular beach.

Explore a cleared village

The walk over rough moorland to Stiomrabhaigh from the remote settlement of Orasaigh may convince you that no one could ever have lived in this forbidding environment. However a quick look around the location high above the lochside reveals the remains of sturdy stone-built dwellings, the telltale ridges of lazy beds, where potatoes and barley would have been grown, the near landscape green against the brown, heather-clad hillside hinting at the cultivation and animal husbandry of the past. In fact, eighty-one people lived in Stiomrabhaigh in sixteen houses in 1851. Eight years later the whole village had been cleared by the landowner to make way for deer. Later the settlement was inhabited again before finally being abandoned in the 1940s. More recently, much of this area, Pairc, has been purchased by the local community who are now in charge of their own land.

Climb Mealaisbhal

Hiking to the highest point on Lewis is worth it for the journey to the start alone. Sitting proud of the other Uig hills on the far west of the island, Mealaisbhal has to be sought out. The journey passes the sandy beaches of Uig and Mangersta, continuing through scattered crofting townships well beyond the tourist trail. The start from Breanais is unprepossessing – heading directly towards the looming hill on an old peat-cutting track which soon deteriorates into a bog. Reaching the rock-strewn slopes of the hill is a relief and the climb gradually rewards with ever-expanding views. From the 574-metre summit the Uig sands, surrounding mountains and watery landscape lie beneath. Expect to be up and down in around four hours. Hardened hillwalkers keen on rocky, pathless scrambling can climb Mealaisbhal as part of a very tough circuit of the Uig hills.

1 Lewis, cleared village of Stiomrabhaigh   **2 Lewis,** west side coast walk   **3 Lewis,** Uig Sands
4 Lewis, heading towards Mealaisbhal   **5 Lewis,** Mealaisbhal summit view

Attend a Gaelic psalm service

Lewis and Harris have a very high level of church attendance – and sabbath observance – compared to the Scottish mainland, and while these traditions are changing fast, Sunday is still a quiet day with very few shops open. The Free Church of Scotland is the main church here, followed by the Church of Scotland and the Free Presbyterian Church of Scotland. Many will hold a Gaelic service in the morning and an English service in the evening, and unaccompanied Gaelic psalm singing is a unique and remarkable experience. Visitors are welcome to attend services – community noticeboards will often give the times – although you should ask locally what is required in the way of dress code as smart clothes and hats are still expected at many churches.

Shuck a scallop

Sampling local, fresh seafood is a must during any visit to the Outer Hebrides. Much of the catch makes its way to mainland Europe and with restaurants far flung in this remote community it's not always easy to source despite the number of creel pots and tiny fishing boats seen around the coast. Luckily the Scallop Shack on Uig pier provides a steady stream of ultra-fresh scallops, mussels and oysters prepared for you to take away and cook. Open all year, the shack also has a cafe serving lunches and takeaways in the summer months – dig in!

Eilean Chaluim Cille

One of at least three Scottish islands bearing this name – which means 'the isle of St Columba' – this one is a tidal isle at the entrance to Loch Erisort on Lewis and is best reached from Cromor in South Lochs.

Discover the ruins of   St Columba's Church

Check the tide times as the causeway to Eilean Chaluim Cille is only crossable for a couple of hours either side of low tide and make sure you leave plenty of time to complete the two-kilometre each way walk from Cromor. Start by taking the track towards the island, passing a number of houses before crossing the causeway, often slippery with seaweed. Once on the green and fertile island bear left to visit the remains of the ancient monastery and church. It is thought that St Columba's followers first built a church on this site around AD 800. The site certainly retains a tranquil and spiritual atmosphere to this day, even though your only companions on this now uninhabited island are likely to be sheep.

Great Bernera

Four thousand people turned up to walk across to Great Bernera when the bridge was opened in 1953. Known as *Beàrnaraigh Mòr* in Gaelic, the island is often referred to simply Bernera or Beàrnaraigh, and the fact that a bridge was built at all was testament to the spirit of the inhabitants who had threatened to take matters into their own hands with a plan to blow up the cliffs to form a causeway. Today's easy access means the island has a sustainable population and a future to match its long history of habitation dating back to Viking times.

1 **Great Bernera,** Bostadh roundhouse

Visit the Bostadh roundhouse 🜨 🌊

In addition to the large standing stone and ancient broch that greet you as you come over the bridge, a large Iron Age settlement lies preserved at the spectacular beach at Bostadh. Uncovered by a storm and since reburied, a replica roundhouse has been built nearby. It can be visited from a nearby parking spot or as part of a half-day (eleven-kilometre) circular walk from Breacleit. It's easy to imagine yourself back in Pictish times as you descend towards the sea and eventually open the door of the thatched building to explore inside.

Pabbay (Loch Roag)

Actually a linked pair of small islands (Pabaigh Mor and Pabaigh Beag) in Loch Roag, Pabbay has a starring role in *The Chessmen*, one of the books in the Peter May's Lewis trilogy, when a boat chase ends in tragedy in one of the island's caves on the day of the Uig Gala. The gala is a real event taking place each July on Reef beach (Traigh na Beirghe) on Lewis and boat trips often run out to Pabbay during the day – otherwise Seatrek can organise a trip.

1

Harris

Harris is Lewis's rough and ready southern sibling – all mountains, wild bog and vast sandy beaches. While technically not an island in its own right as it's part of the same landmass as Lewis, it is always referred to as the Isle of Harris and has its own distinct geography and culture – and deserves bagging rights of its own. Tarbert, situated at the narrow waist which almost divides Harris in two, is the main centre and this is where the CalMac ferry from Skye docks. There is a hotel, shops and a school here. A recent tourist boom across the Outer Hebrides has increased the accommodation options across the island, but it's always advisable to book in advance in the summer months. A fairly fast road links Tarbert with Lewis to the north, while the ferry on to Berneray leaves from Leverburgh in the south.

Climb An Cliseam

The Harris hills are rough and unforgiving but the ascent of An Cliseam (Clisham) – the highest in the Outer Hebrides – is rewarded with stunning views over mountains and endless seas. The 799-metre-high summit is not so far from the road, yet it isn't obtained easily – the most direct route climbs relentlessly across boggy then rocky ground from the A859 and for a fit walker it's possible to get up and down in under four hours. A much more satisfying route, known as the Clisham horseshoe, makes a day-long circuit by approaching via the ridges of Mulla-Fo-Thuath and Mulla-Fo-Dheas. With some scrambling in places, it's regarded as a Hebridean hillwalking classic and definitely not one to miss if you have the necessary skills and experience.

Look out for the Orb

Self-sufficient Harris folk have traditionally spun wool from their sheep and woven it into cloth, using dyes from local plants and lichens and urine to 'fix' the colour (many croft houses would have had a large pisspot outside to collect this valuable asset). After spinning, the cloth would be created on a loom and then the fabric 'waulked' – or finished – by repeatedly soaking and thumping it rhythmically, often by a group of women singing traditional Gaelic 'waulking' songs to keep time. Today, Harris Tweed is still produced by hand and it is world-famous – and protected by the Orb trademark. Look out for signs to modern-day weaving sheds where the production techniques have changed little over the years; many will have lengths of cloth for sale and often finished products in this iconic fabric.

Huisinis beach hunt

Quite possibly the most scenic drive in the Outer Hebrides, the last few miles of single-track B887 from near Tarbert provide stunning views across Loch a Siar to the island of Taransay. The sands at Huisinis (Hushinish) are the main draw, and while this pristine white strand is often completely deserted, there are even more isolated and pristine beaches just waiting to be discovered just out of view. Follow a rough path north from the parking area eventually walking under the imposing flank of Sròn nam Fiadh and alongside Loch na Cleabhaig, passing a lonely cottage before reaching the sandy beach at Crabhadail.

Gawp at the Sheela-na-gig at Rodel church

Found on religious buildings throughout Europe, Sheela-na-gigs are stone-carved female figures pointing to or pulling open their vulvas. It is thought they served the same purpose

1 **Harris**, approaching An Cliseam on the horseshoe   2 **Harris**, tweed   3 **Harris**, An Cliseam summit
4 **Harris**, Huisinis beach   5 **Harris**, Rodel church   6 **Harris**, Sheela-na-gig at Rodel

as grotesques or gargoyles to ward off evil spirits, but the immodesty of the Sheela-na-gig suggests the possible survival of a pagan goddess into Christian times, a fertility symbol or even a warning against the dangers of lust. Make your own mind up as you search out the walls of beautiful and ancient St Clement's church in Rodel for this fine example.

Cycle the golden road 🚲

So called because of the extremely high cost of construction, the 'golden road' runs down the rocky lunar landscape of the east side of Harris from Tarbet to Leverburgh. The project was government funded, partly to provide children with access to schools. The route links a number of tiny coastal settlements on the rough heather and rock moonscape that contrasts so vividly with the sandy coastal strip on the west. Today this quiet switchback road is a cyclist's dream, passing numerous tidal inlets with the chance to get close to otters and eagles. As always in the Outer Hebrides, the weather will decide how arduous the twisty-turny, uppy-downy road will feel from the saddle.

Claim your own stretch of perfection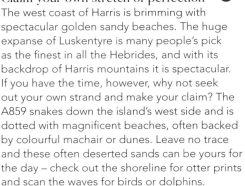

The west coast of Harris is brimming with spectacular golden sandy beaches. The huge expanse of Luskentyre is many people's pick as the finest in all the Hebrides, and with its backdrop of Harris mountains it is spectacular. If you have the time, however, why not seek out your own strand and make your claim? The A859 snakes down the island's west side and is dotted with magnificent beaches, often backed by colourful machair or dunes. Leave no trace and these often deserted sands can be yours for the day – check out the shoreline for otter prints and scan the waves for birds or dolphins.

Scalpay

Joined to Harris by an elegant bridge which opened in 1997, Scalpay is one of a growing number of Scottish islands owned by its residents, in this case thanks to the previous owner who gifted the island to the community. Blessed by two great natural harbours, Scalpay has traditionally been an island of fishermen,

with an equally thriving female-driven knitting industry. In recent decades fishing has declined in importance and the replacement of the ferry by the bridge has seen more people move to the island, making it easier to commute to Tarbert or elsewhere. Approximately 300 people currently live on the island, many of them in or around North Harbour (An Acairsaid a Tuath). The interior is rugged and dotted with lochans. Scalpay has a bed and breakfast, a number of self-catering options and two cafes.

Visit the first lighthouse in these isles

The first lighthouse to be built on the Outer Hebrides, Eilean Glas stands at the far south-east corner of Scalpay. You can still see the stump of the original lighthouse, built in 1789 but replaced less than forty years later by the red-and-white-striped Stevenson tower that stands today. You can visit it as part of a circular ten-kilometre hike around Scalpay, following rough waymarkers and exploring moorland lochans as well the island's highest point with views to Skye on a clear day.

Tickle your taste buds at the North Harbour Bistro and Tearoom

With so much fine seafood being caught by fishermen from this island it would be shame to leave without sampling some of it. This friendly bistro and tearoom is the place to do it. In addition to seafood, the imaginative cooking – think *Masterchef* final without the presenters' gurning – really showcases the local produce. Booking is essential for evenings, but they also rustle up a mean soup and scone at lunchtime.

Taransay

Taransay is best known for its starring role in the early reality TV show *Castaway 2000* when thirty-six people were tasked with building a community on this small island just three kilometres off the Harris coast. Owned by the Borve Lodge Estate, it is possible to visit by kayak or private charter; Seatrek, based on Lewis, occasionally runs trips here.

The island once supported a number of crofters in three settlements but the last family left in 1974. Since then there have been no

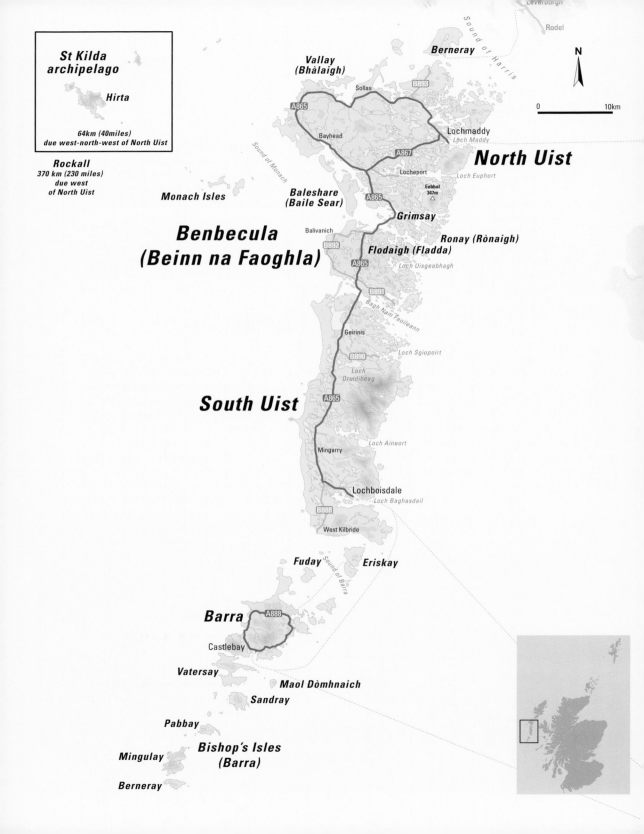

St Kilda
archipelago

Hirta

64km (40miles)
due west-north-west of North Uist

Rockall
370 km (230 miles)
due west
of North Uist

Monach Isles

*Benbecula
(Beinn na Faoghla)*

*Baleshare
(Baile Sear)*

South Uist

Barra

Vatersay

Maol Dòmhnaich

Sandray

Pabbay

Mingulay

*Bishop's Isles
(Barra)*

Berneray

*Valley
(Bhàlaigh)*

Sollas

Bayhead

B893

A865

A867

Lochmaddy
Loch Maddy

Locheport

Loch Euphort

North Uist

Eabhal
347m

Grimsay

Ronay (Rònaigh)

Flodaigh (Fladda)

Balivanich

B892

A865

Loch Uisgeabhagh

B891

Bagh Nam Faoileann

Geirinis

B890

Loch Sgiopoirt

*Loch
Druidibeag*

A865

Loch Aineort

Mingarry

Lochboisdale
Loch Baghasdail

B888

West Kilbride

Fuday

Sound of Barra

Eriskay

A888

Castlebay

Sound of Harris

Leverburgh

Rodel

Berneray

N

0   10km

Sound of Monach

permanent residents except a herd of red deer, large bird populations and sheep grazed here. In addition to the more modern properties you can still see the remains of two ancient burial chapels at Paible. The island is almost split in two, a narrow strip of land joining the two sections both of which have a notable small hill and a number of sandy bays backed by machair awash with flowers in early summer.

Scarp

The number of buildings still standing on Scarp is testament to the thriving community that once lived here. Lying just off the west coast of Harris and only a short distance from Huisinis, Scarp has been uninhabited since 1971; the maintained houses are now used as summer holiday homes. The narrow strait was the site of a postal experiment in 1943 when German inventor Gerhard Zucker used rockets to deliver mail over the sea to the island. As the singed remains of letters rained down, it became apparent this was not a permanent replacement for the local waterborne postie. Lacking a rocket launcher, the only way to reach Scarp today is by boat or kayak.

Pabbay

A few kilometres west of Leverburgh on Harris, Pabbay is a low-lying green island with some amazing sandy beaches. So fertile it became known as the 'granary of Harris', it was once home to over 300 people before being cleared to make way for sheep by 1846. It is now uninhabited. Pabbay residents were renowned as skilled illicit distillers, putting their ample barley crops to good use and working alongside the ferrymen on Bernera who would hoist a warning flag if they had excisemen on

board so as to give time for evidence to be hidden. However, a successful raid provided evidence then used by the landlord's factor as the basis for the later evictions, eventually leaving only one shepherd and family on the island. The ruins of houses can still be seen amidst the grazing sheep and deer. It is possible to charter a boat from Seatrek on Lewis.

Flannan Isles

This small group of islands – also known as the Seven Hunters – lies thirty-four kilometres north-west of Gallan Head on the Lewis coast. Visits are only possible through private charters, but there is no sheltered anchorage for yachts.

The largest island, Eilean Mòr, is home to the Flannan Isles lighthouse, itself the setting for an enduring mystery. Just before Christmas 1900 the three lighthouse keepers seemingly vanished off the face of the earth with no obvious explanation. The disappearance spawned a cottage industry in theories including abduction by pirates, being eaten by seabirds or a cabin-fever quarrel that got out of hand. More recent historians suggest that stormy seas and an accident were most likely to blame, but no remains have ever been recovered. The lighthouse was automated in 1971 which is when the last residents left.

St Kilda Archipelago

Scotland's *Ultima Thule*, St Kilda is at the top of many island baggers' wish lists, with the long, long journey west to the isolated island group over eighty kilometres west of Harris becoming something of a pilgrimage.

There are now many day trips to the islands, most of which allow between four and five hours ashore on the largest island, Hirta, together with a cruise around Boreray and its great stacks. The fastest crossing from Leverburgh on Harris takes around two hours each way, but many of the boats are slower and actual journey times depend on the weather and any stops for wildlife viewing. Go to St Kilda operates trips from Stein on Skye.

All trips to St Kilda are prone to cancellation due to poor weather so it is best to be flexible with your plans. Some operators will arrange longer trips allowing stays at the basic campsite at Village Bay which is run by the custodians of St Kilda, the National Trust for Scotland. It is also possible to spend a week or longer as a volunteer with the Trust undertaking conservation work.

Top out on Hirta

On a clear day, climbing to the highest point of the archipelago is a fantastic way to appreciate the isolation of St Kilda, experiencing the immensity of its cliffs and imagining the hardships of scratching a living from them.

Once ashore, head right from the pier, skirting round the army base buildings and aiming uphill, passing a number of stone-built cleits or shelters used by the St Kildans to store peats, eggs and other foodstuffs. Aim for The Gap where suddenly the climb gives way to a cliff plunging 150 metres vertically to the sea. The residents of St Kilda were skilled climbers who used these cliffs to catch seabirds for food and oil and also to collect eggs. From The Gap continue to the left, heading up steep ground populated with often angry nesting bonxies (great skuas) in the summer months, to eventually reach the summit of Conachair (430 metres). The stone trig point teeters frighteningly close to the sheer cliff edge – Conachair has the highest sea cliff in all Britain – and the view out to Boreray and its stacks is unique.

A 200-metre detour leads to a second trig point which gives an aerial view of Village Bay and the neat row of houses occupied until the island was evacuated in 1930. The quickest descent is to take the track down from the Ministry of Defence station to leave enough time to explore the poignant remains of the village, museum, church and schoolroom.

Join the St Kilda parliament

Every day the men of St Kilda would line the main street for their parliament meeting where the day's activities would be decided on and any matters of discord in the community resolved – presumably while the women got on with work. Everyone was free to speak and there was no one in charge – decisions had to be agreed upon. Various visitors from Martin Martin in 1697 onwards, including a steady stream of intrepid 'tourists' in Victorian times, recorded that there were few long-term divisions in the St Kildan society and that no serious crimes had been committed.

The last residents were evacuated from St Kilda in 1930 at their own request, the population having been ravaged by a combination of disease and emigration. The last person to be born on St Kilda died in 2016 although descendants still visit. Today you can wander into many of the ruined houses – look out for the pebbles placed near the fireplaces that record the names of the last inhabitants.

Spot the St Kilda wren

The island group's isolation from the rest of Scotland means it has become something of an evolutionary test case, a more northerly and considerably more bracing Galápagos.

1 **St Kilda (Hirta)**, Boreray, from Conachair   2 **St Kilda (Hirta)**, looking over Village Bay from Conachair
3 **St Kilda**, Stac Lee, Boreray   4 and 5 **St Kilda (Hirta)**, the houses of Village Bay

Keen-eyed island baggers may be lucky enough to spot the St Kilda wren, which has adapted to life on the island and is different enough from its mainland cousins to qualify as its own sub-species (*Troglodytes troglodytes hirtensis* to give it its Sunday name). While slightly larger than a normal wren, it is also greyer with more obvious stripy markings but is still hard to spot as it flits amongst the stones and cleits on the island. There's also a St Kilda mouse.

See the great stacks of Boreray

Stac an Armin and Stac Lee project from the sea near the tiny island of Boreray like sharks' fins. Housing an unfathomable number of seabirds, the stacks present a whirling mass of feathers when viewed from the sea during the nesting season. The stacks are the highest in Britain, and both are Marilyns (hills with a relative drop of 150 metres all the way round),

presenting perhaps the ultimate challenge to hill baggers. Getting ashore, let alone climbing up the guano-covered rock, is a very serious undertaking, and given the protected status of this National Nature Reserve is only permitted outside the bird nesting season.

Boreray is the smallest Scottish island to have a summit over a thousand feet high – Mullach an Eilein, at 384 metres – and it appears as a great mountain rising sheer from the sea. Landing is difficult, yet incredibly there are prehistoric remains that suggest an early farming community survived here. In more modern times, eleven St Kildans were marooned on the island over winter in 1727 when a smallpox epidemic meant there was no one able to row over to rescue the group which had been left on Boreray to undertake a fowling trip.

Cruising round the stacks and Boreray is an

incredible experience, visiting these fearsome cliffs up close and marvelling at the St Kildans who regularly climbed the stacks hunting fulmar, gannets and other seabirds, and collecting eggs.

Rockall

This tiny block of granite projecting from the open Atlantic lies over 300 kilometres further west even than St Kilda. It was first claimed by the UK in 1955 when two marines and a naturalist raised a flag on the rock and affixed a plaque – though this has long gone. It became part of Scotland in 1972, although Ireland has never recognised the UK's claim.

Fewer than twenty people have ever set foot on Rockall, and it remains a magnet for eccentric adventurers and the most extreme of island baggers. Explorer Nick Hancock managed to survive forty-three days on it in 2014, breaking the previous solo record of forty days set by a former member of the SAS in 1985.

It is hard to imagine a more forbidding place than this bare rock out of all sight of any other land. For most island baggers it remains forever just a dream – or perhaps a nightmare.

North Rona

Actually just named Rona, it is often referred to as North Rona to distinguish this isolated island from the Rona off the coast of Skye. Lying seventy-seven kilometres north of the Butt of Lewis it is seriously remote, the perfect spot for the medieval hermits who came to live here, following in the footsteps of St Ronan who is thought to have stayed in the eighth century. Life would certainly have been tough, and there

is evidence that at one point in the seventeenth century the population died out from a combination of starvation and the plague.

Shepherds clung on as residents until 1844 when the owner made an offer of the island for use as penal colony. This was declined by the government, and the island has remained uninhabited ever since. It is possible to make the long journey by chartering a boat, and Seatrek will sometimes run trips although landing can never be guaranteed. Exploring the grassy island on foot is relatively easy once ashore and the remains of settlements and the chapel are easy to make out.

Sula Sgeir

Sula is the Norse word for gannet and it is this elegant seabird that dominates and makes its home on the tiny rocky island of Sula Sgeir, sixty-four kilometres north of the Butt of Lewis. For centuries men from Ness have journeyed out to this remote rock to hunt the juvenile gannets, or guga, for their meat and feathers. This controversial tradition carries on today under a special licence issued by the Scottish Government. The resulting guga meat is highly prized by those who have acquired the taste – heavily salted, it is best accompanied by a large glass of milk. As the hunt is limited to 2,000 birds, the guga meat is rationed and sold on the quayside when the annual hunt boat returns. It is possible to visit Sula Sgeir by chartered boat, often in combination with a longer trip to North Rona. If a visit is not possible, watching the fascinating 2011 documentary *The Guga Hunters of Ness* will give you an insight into the local tradition as well as many views of the forbidding island scenery.

1 St Kilda, Boreray

Shiant Islands

The Shiants are a group of small islands renowned for their seabirds, and lie approximately seven kilometres from the Lewis coast in the Minch, the waters between Skye and the Outer Hebrides. Geologically a continuation of the Trotternish Ridge on Skye, the rock is volcanic and forms some impressively high sea cliffs providing a natural haven for seabirds, particularly puffins and razorbills as well as Manx shearwaters and European storm petrels.

Getting to the Shiants usually involves a private charter from either Skye or Lewis unless you have your own boat or kayak. There is a bothy on the island which is available for visitors to stay in with the arrangement of the owner, Tom Nicolson. Tom's father, Adam, wrote a fine book about the islands called *Sea Room*, as well as a more recent discussion about the future of our seabirds and oceans, *The Seabird's Cry*. *www.shiantisles.net*

Berneray

The only inhabited island in the Sound of Harris, Berneray is linked to North Uist via a causeway which was opened in 1999, and to Leverburgh on Harris by a CalMac ferry. Berneray supports a population of around 130, most involved in crofting. There is a shop, cafe and post office, as well as a community centre, two hostels and a number of bed and breakfast and self-catering options. In the summer, the old Nurses Cottage houses displays on history, ancestry, crofting and wildlife, as well as information about facilities on the island – follow the east road to find it.

Stay in a blackhouse

The picturesque hostel on Berneray is run by the Hebrides-based Gatliff Hebridean Hostels Trust. Converted from a traditional blackhouse, it's actually painted white. *Dubh* is Gaelic for black and some say the name comes from the dark interior and peat, but it could also be a corruption from *tughadh* which means

1 Berneray, hostel   **2** Berneray, causeway to North Uist   **3** Berneray, Beinn Sleibhe

'thatched', and used to differentiate from the more modern harled 'white houses' that often replaced the blackhouses. These dwellings would have housed the family at one end and their livestock partitioned off at the other, providing a source of warmth in the winter. The hostel sits right on the beach and is a wonderful place to swap island tales with other travellers.

Watch for otters from the causeway

The first thing to notice as you approach the causeway to Berneray is the *Caution Otters Crossing* road sign. When the causeway was built in the late 1990s several underwater otter runs were incorporated in the structure to allow the otters to pass through – but you still need to watch out for any on the road. Almost anywhere on the coast of Berneray is good for otter spotting, and they are most likely to be seen on a rising tide. Scan the water for the telltale V-shape created as they swim. They often come ashore to eat crab, butterfish or some other tasty prey, but are easy to lose amongst the kelp and rocks. Their footprints in the sand are also a giveaway as otters have five toes in comparison

with a dog's four. Keep binoculars handy, and if you do fail to spot this elusive creature check out the otter sculpture on the roof of the thatched hostel.

Climb Beinn Shleibhe

Much of Berneray is low-lying, fertile machair. For the best view climb to the trig point atop Beinn Shleibhe from where there are panoramic views over the whole island as well as nearby Pabbay and the mountains of Harris. Climbing this ninety-three-metre high point can easily be incorporated into a circular walk around Berneray which can also include the impressive Cladh Maolrithe standing stone.

Visit the great West Beach

No visit to Berneray is complete without a frolic on the stunning sands of the five-kilometre-long West Beach – so good they were once used by the Thai tourist office to promote their own beaches. Start from the community hall and head out, passing some prehistoric remains including an ancient souterrain before crossing the machair and dunes to reach the beach.

1 North Uist, Eaval **2** North Uist, view from Eaval

North Uist

A remarkable watery landscape of blue, green and purple, North Uist consists of peat moorland dotted with innumerable lochans and bog. In fact, over half the 'landmass' is covered with water, and the divide between salt and freshwater is frequently unclear.

The main settlement Lochmaddy is linked by CalMac vehicle ferry to Uig on Skye. North Uist is also linked by causeway to Berneray in the north (from where a ferry runs to Leverburgh on Harris), and to Benbecula via Grimsay in the south. Most of the shops and accommodation, which includes a hotel, is in Lochmaddy, as well as Taigh Chearsabhagh, a fine arts centre and museum. There are self-catering cottages to rent dotted around the island.

See no Eaval

An ascent of Eaval is the perfect introduction to the watery landscape of North Uist. The bird's-eye view from the summit of this conical hill looks down on a maze of tiny lochans and larger sea lochs. The route starts from the end of the road heading along the south side of Loch Euphort. The often-wet approach soon runs alongside Loch Obasaraigh, crossing an outflow that can be impassable at the highest tides. There are good views to the cone-shaped Eaval and the climb soon begins in earnest, eventually reaching the trig point and shelter cairn marking the 347-metre summit; it boasts a unique view that will never be forgotten.

Try peat-smoked salmon from the Hebridean Smokehouse

The Hebridean Smokehouse has been combining the flavours of salmon and peat smoke for almost thirty years. A truly locally produced food, the fish and shellfish all comes from the waters surrounding North Uist, while the peat is locally cut. As well as salmon, sea trout, scallops and other shellfish, the smokehouse also produces a salmon smoked using old whisky barrels and finished with a sprinkling of the water of life itself – try it with an oat cake and smear of soft crowdie cheese. The smokehouse can be found on the west side of the island at Clachan. *www.hebrideansmokehouse.com*

Meet Finn's people at   North Uist's ancient sites

There are a number of ancient chambered cairns in the Uists but Barpa Langass is by far the most impressive. A massive pile of stones covers three chambers, thought to have been used for the burial of an important tribe rather than just a select few individuals. Although the narrow entrance can still be made out, recent collapses mean the structure is now too dangerous to enter. While here be sure to walk to the nearby and incredibly atmospheric Pobull Fhinn stone circle. Overlooking Loch Langais, the stones date back at least 3,000 years. The path from the cairn to the stone circle continues past the Langass Lodge Hotel from where it is possible to complete the circuit by heading back up to the main road and turning right.

Listen for the corncrake's rasp   at Balranald

Often heard but rarely seen, the corncrake is a summer visitor to North Uist and the RSPB reserve at Balranald is one of the best places to try and spot this elusive bird. Related to the moorhen and only slightly bigger than a blackbird, the brown, slightly striped corncrake has bright brown wings and long legs and tends to hide in the nettles and flag iris that dot the crofts of North Uist. The RSPB runs evening walks where you are most likely to hear the bird's unmistakable rasping call or catch a glimpse. Even if you don't spot a corncrake, Balranald is a fantastic place to walk – follow marker cairns to the most westerly point, the Aird an Runair peninsula.

1 North Uist, Hut of the Shadows **2** North Uist, smoking salmon **Photo:** Hebridean Smokehouse **3** North Uist, Sanctuary – on the Uist sculpture trail **4** North Uist, beach at Balranald RSPB reserve **5** Valley, crossing the tidal sands **6** Valley, ruins

The Uist Sculpture Trail

Spend a day hunting for these seven sculptures dotted across the island. Commissioned by the Taigh Chearsabhagh museum and arts centre in Lochmaddy, all the artworks interact with the natural environment, including High Tide, Low Tide where the sea slowly draws salt from a dome situated on rocks in the intertidal zone of the shore. This piece and Mosaic Mackerel, a large fish sculpture incorporating mussel and other shells, are close to the arts centre, while the others, including an intriguing camera obscura called Hut of the Shadows, require a bit more exploring to find.

Beachcomb at Clachan Sands

Traigh Hornais ranks amongst the finest of the stunning sandy beaches in the Outer Hebrides. Backed by dunes, the sparkling turquoise waters look tropical on a sunny day – until you dip your toe in the bracing waves. Unless you're feeling very brave, leave the swimming to the dolphins, seals and the occasional otter that sometimes ride the waves. Access the beach on foot from the Hornais cemetery; bear left at the sands to pass a much older burial ground and eventually reach the headland at the end of the beach where there is a good view to the island of Orasaigh.

Vallay (Bhàlaigh)

Now uninhabited, this tiny tidal island is still farmed as well as being run as a nature reserve by the RSPB, but it was once home to over fifty people. The impressive ruins that dominate the island were once the very grand Vallay House, built in the early twentieth century by the industrialist and amateur archaeologist Erskine Beveridge. After Beveridge's death in 1920 the house was left to his son, but was later abandoned after he drowned in the waters here in 1944.

Cross the tidal sands to the island (Bhàlaigh)

With bare feet, a keen eye on the tide times and a sense of adventure, the hike over to Vallay is a fabulous experience. Start from Aird Glas just west of Malacleit on North Uist and leave enough time to cross to the far side of the island where there is a sandy beach and headland with the remains of an ancient chapel. Only undertake this at the start of low tide and in fine weather – the water rushes back in extremely quickly and there are deeper, dangerous channels, so leave plenty of time to return safely (and warm up your feet!).

1 and **2 Bebencula**, Rueval summit   **3** Grey seal   **4** Grey seal pup   **5 South Uist**, beach near Hallan

Baleshare (Baile Sear)

Linked to North Uist by a causeway since 1962, Baleshare is a low-lying island so flat it doesn't even warrant a contour line on the Ordnance Survey's Landranger map, rising to only twelve metres at its highest point. However it does boast a spectacular white sandy beach backed by dunes. The causeway has helped to preserve the crofting lifestyle here, with around fifty residents continuing a history of habitation stretching back to prehistoric times. Acting as a buffer protecting North Uist from the Atlantic, coastal erosion has eaten away at Baleshare over the centuries, and it is said that until a seventeenth-century storm it was possible at low tide to walk to the Monach Isles fourteen kilometres away.

Monach Isles

This group of islands, also known as Heisker (*Heisgeir* in Gaelic), lie west from the North Uist coast. The main three islands, Ceann Iar, Shivinish and Ceann Ear, are thought to have once been a single island but the coastal erosion that also took away the land bridge that until the seventeenth century linked the Monachs to Baleshare also separated these islands.

Low-lying and once crofted by over a hundred inhabitants, the islands are now a National Nature Reserve famed for their flower-rich carpet of machair and one of the largest breeding colonies of grey seals in the world. There is a Stevenson lighthouse on the smaller island of Shillay. Getting to the Monachs usually requires your own boat or charter, though Lady Anne Boat Trips based on Grimsay sometimes offers day trips.

Grimsay

Grimsay lies between North Uist and Benbecula, and has been crossed by a road and causeways between these two islands since 1960. Previously it had to be reached either by boat or a hazardous tidal ford.

Learn a traditional craft

Grimsay has long been a centre of traditional boatbuilding and there is a boatyard at Kallin. If you don't have the time to learn to craft an entire boat, check out the beautiful boat shed and nearby museum. If boatbuilding isn't your thing, why not master spinning at Uist Wool? Here you can learn about the entire process required to transform sheep's wool into stylish garments.

Ronay (Rònaigh)

Lying to the east of Grimsay, privately owned Ronay is a rugged island of small, rounded, heather-clad peaks, with a complex, deeply indented coastline. There is a self-catering property available for weekly lets, although you will need to hire a boat to take you across – or kayak or sail there under your own steam. Cleared for sheep farming in the 1820s, the island once had a population of 180.

Benbecula (Beinn na Faoghla)

Lying between North Uist and South Uist, and with a name deriving from 'pennyland of the fords' in Gaelic, is Benbecula. Before the

causeways which link these islands were built, it would have been necessary to ford the tidal sands between the land masses. Now, as well as the causeways which link to North Uist via Grimsay, and to South Uist, the island has its own airport with direct flights from Glasgow, Stornoway and Barra. The main settlement is Balivanich, which has shops, a post office, a cafe and a small hospital. The annual Eilean Dorcha Festival takes place on the island in July featuring an eclectic mix of traditional music, rock and pop, and even the occasional tribute band.

Reveal the whole island from Rueval (Ruabhal)

Top out on the diminutive summit of Rueval to get a true understanding of the watery moorland landscape of the Dark Island – An t-Eilean Dorcha – as Benbecula is sometimes known. From the island's highest point at 124 metres an expanse of loch and rock is spread out beneath you. On a clear day the jagged mountains of the Skye Cuillin can be made out across the Minch. It was this thirty-nine-kilometre stretch of water that Flora MacDonald rowed with Bonnie Prince Charlie during his escape after defeat at Culloden in 1746, getting blown ashore at Rosinish, seen to the east from Rueval's summit. The ascent starts from near a recycling centre on the A865 in the centre of the island, and it forms part of the Hebridean Way long-distance walk.

Know your oats

Oatcakes are a Scottish institution and particularly popular in the Outer Hebrides. The three brothers of Macleans bakery have been producing the savoury biscuits here since 1987, and they are sold widely throughout Scotland. Check out the bakery shop in Uachdar and try one with local crowdie or smoked salmon – but, be warned: oatcakes are very addictive and go well with practically any topping!

Flodaigh (Fladda)

Originally a tidal island, Flodaigh is now linked to Benbecula by a causeway – though this island is a dead end. Its 145 hectares are crofted by a population of around ten, and stepping ashore can feel like stepping back in time by a generation.

Sing with the seals

It's all about the seals that haul out on rocks and generally hang out in a large sheltered bay on the east of this small island. To reach the seals it's best to aim for low tide and follow a track on foot to the right after the causeway, heading through a couple of gates and following signs to reach the shore. While grey seals dominate here there are also signs of otters and the patient and keen-eyed may be rewarded with a sighting.

South Uist

More than 1,700 people – known as *Deasaich*, or 'southerners' – live scattered around South Uist. Most of them reside in settlements along the flatter fertile strip of machair on the west which is lined by seemingly endless beaches. To the east is a complete contrast as the island rises to a rugged mountain range.

South Uist is linked to Benbecula in the north – and from there on to North Uist – by a causeway, and also to Eriskay in the south. CalMac ferries run from the main settlement, Lochboisdale, to Mallaig and Oban on the mainland, as well as to the island of Barra. Lochboisdale was a major fishing port during the nineteenth-century herring boom and today has a hotel, a couple of shops, cafe and garage. Accommodation of all types is scattered across the length of South Uist.

Fish finger food

Hot-smoked salmon is a unique taste that should not be missed during a visit to South Uist. Smoked in small batches in traditional hand-built kilns, the flaky salmon has a distinctive and delicious taste quite different from traditional cold-smoked salmon. Located in the north of the island, the Salar smokehouse overlooks the water and the pier where fishing boats tie up – a small shop means you'll be prepared for a true Hebridean picnic. *www.salarsmokehouse.co.uk*

Hang out at Howmore hostel

The Gatliff Hebridean Hostels Trust has converted one of this cluster of thatched blackhouses into a basic, atmospheric hostel. Sited on the machair only a stone's throw from the sea, the tiny building neighbours the remains of a thirteenth-century monastery. Sleeping sixteen in four dormitories, the friendly hostel is a great way to meet other travellers and is popular with those undertaking the Hebridean Way on foot or by bike.

Raise the Saltire at Flora MacDonald's house

Flora MacDonald was born nearby and was brought up at the spot marked by this ruin and memorial. While only the parts of the cottage walls remain, the large memorial erected by Clan MacDonald and the wide sweeping views make this an atmospheric pilgrimage to the Jacobite cause. Flora herself was rather a reluctant activist, persuaded by friends to aid the Stuart heir. She helped Bonnie Prince Charlie – dressed as her maid – escape to Skye from Uist in a rowing boat following his defeat at the Battle of Culloden in 1746, a feat later immortalised in the Skye Boat Song.

1 South Uist, Howmore blackhouses   **2 South Uist**, Salar hot-smoked salmon
3 South Uist, pony at Loch Druidibeg   **4 South Uist**, Cladh Hallan roundhouse

Climb Beinn Mhor

The ascent of South Uist's highest mountain is a serious hillwalking challenge requiring a full day and competent navigation skills. Start from the A865 just north of Loch Dobhrain and take the track used to access the peat cuttings heading directly for three distant mountains – once beyond this the going is rough and pathless. Beinn Mhor means 'big mountain', yet is actually only 620 metres above sea level. The summit is reached along a spectacular ridge and is blessed with fantastic views. Enthusiastic hillwalkers often combine the ascent with Hecla and Beinn Corradail to make a Hebridean classic.

Play a round on Tom Morris's course at Askernish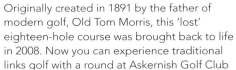

Originally created in 1891 by the father of modern golf, Old Tom Morris, this 'lost' eighteen-hole course was brought back to life in 2008. Now you can experience traditional links golf with a round at Askernish Golf Club

– look out for the corncrake on the club's logo. Ecological management techniques, including a ban on herbicides, have helped protect the fragile machair environment, and the continued use of the course for cattle and sheep grazing in the winter has earned the club the moniker 'the most natural golf course in the world'. Clubs and trolleys are available for hire.

Take in a roundhouse at Cladh Hallan

A short walk near Dalabrog brings you to the remains of three large early Bronze Age roundhouses. The sunken circles and remains of the stone walls can be clearly seen. It is thought people lived in these dwellings between 1100 BC and AD 200, making them rank amongst the longest inhabited prehistoric houses in the world. Several burials have been excavated here including a mummified man and woman. It is possible to make a longer circular walk by heading on to the spectacular sandy beach and returning via the machair.

Walk on water at Loch Druidibeg

Paths including sections of boardwalk enable you to explore this watery landscape. A circular walk taking in four lochs and the contrasting sandy coastal machair gives the best chance of seeing the wide range of birdlife and the free-roaming ponies living here. Designated a National Nature Reserve, this rare habitat is now managed by local community organisation Stòras Uibhist, owners of a large part of the island following one of the first large-scale community buyouts of land in Scotland. Stòras Uibhist also owns Eriskay to the south, and parts of Benbecula.

Bag a remote bothy at Uisinis

Considered one of the most remote bothies in Scotland, Uisinis is an open shelter for walkers, nestled against the mountain of Hecla behind and overlooking the sea. Maintained by the Mountain Bothies Association, this simple shelter, furnished with a stove, sleeping platform and a couple of chairs, provides a real get-away-from-it-all retreat. Take all your own gear – including fuel, unless you are going to take a chance on finding driftwood on the pebbly shore.

Catch a mobile movie at the Screen Machine

With the nearest cinema in faraway Stornoway, a night at the movies in this part of the Outer Hebrides may feel unlikely. However, every ten weeks or so, the eighteen-wheeled truck that is the Screen Machine mobile cinema rocks up on South Uist and in many other places around the Highlands and Islands. The sides of the wagon slide out to reveal an eighty-seater cinema which shows the latest releases, although you do have to bring your own popcorn. Watch out for posters showing where it will be next, or book online: *www.screenmachine.co.uk*

Eriskay

Lying offshore from South Uist but connected by a causeway, Eriskay is a real gem. Traditionally a crofting and fishing community, tourism now bolsters the economy although a number of fishing boats still run out of Acarseid Mhòr on the sheltered east side of the island. Just under 150 people live here, and there is a supermarket, cafe, pub which serves food, a bed and breakfast and a couple of

1 Eriskay, from the slopes of Beinn Sciathan **2 Eriskay,** Coilleag a'Phrionnsa

self-catering cottages. Locals took control of the island when it was part of a larger community buyout by Stòras Uibhist in 2006.

Eriskay is linked to South Uist by a causeway, the last one to be built in the Outer Hebrides and opened in 2001. Since then the island has become the main CalMac vehicle ferry link connecting the Uists to Barra – a forty-minute journey south from Eriskay.

Climb to the highest point for 360-degree views

The hike to the 186-metre summit of Ben Scrien (Beinn Sciathan) may be short but it's also very rough, pathless and steep. The reward is a fabulous all-round view of Eriskay and its neighbours. Although other walkers are rare, you are likely to encounter Eriskay ponies, a hardy breed endemic to the Hebrides with a thick waterproof coat – something you are also likely to find useful here.

Sample Whisky Galore

Am Politician is the place for a dram and a tale. Just offshore from here the *SS Politician* floundered and ran aground in rough seas in 1941. Locals rushed out in boats to liberate,

or rescue, the cargo which included a large number of whisky bottles, many of which were secreted away across the island. The episode was immortalised – and exaggerated – in Compton Mackenzie's *Whisky Galore*, which was later made into a successful Ealing comedy (recently remade). Today you can see one of the original bottles, with some of its whisky still inside, behind the bar of Am Politician.

Visit Bonnie Prince Charlie's beach

This stunning strip of white sand just north of the ferry terminal is the place where Bonnie Prince Charlie first set foot on Scottish soil. Arriving from France in July 1745 he received scant support initially from local clans, soon moving on to the mainland where he raised his standard at Glenfinnan and began the Jacobite rebellion. Today the beach is named Coilleag a'Phrionnsa, meaning the 'prince's cockleshell strand'; you'll often have it to yourself. Check out the sandy ground at the back of the beach for the low-growing white and pink flower, sea bindweed – the only place it is found in the Outer Hebrides. It is said that it grows here because seeds fell from the Young Pretender's pockets as he came ashore.

Barra

On a fine summer's day there are few islands that can compete with Barra for its sheer beauty, with steep hills, machair rich in wild flowers, and perfect beaches. Together with its neighbour Vatersay – to which it is linked by a causeway – it is home to just over a thousand people. Most of the facilities are centred around Castlebay, which has a shop, cafe/bistro, hotels and a hostel. There's also a hotel by Halaman Bay. Tourism is now a major contributor to the island economy, although fishing and fish processing remain important, together with crofting.

Barra can be reached by a long CalMac ferry ride from Oban on the mainland, or a shorter run from either Eriskay or Lochboisdale on South Uist. Regular flights from Glasgow touch down on the beach runaway, providing an unforgettable approach to the island. There is a good bus service which trundles around the circular main road on Barra and also across the causeway to Vatersay.

Look over the shoulder of Our Lady of the Sea

Barra, like South Uist, is predominantly Catholic – a contrast to the strong Protestant tradition on Harris and Lewis at the opposite end of the island chain. The large white statue of Madonna and Child stands on the flanks of the island's highest peak, Heaval, and provides an aerial view of Castlebay directly below. Erected in 1954, the best way to reach it is to take the main island road north-east from Castlebay to a parking area at the shoulder of the hill. From here a rough path makes the extremely steep but grassy ascent. Having already climbed to the statue you may as well continue up the steep slopes to the summit of Heaval; the 360-degree views of the island and encircling ocean are awe-inspiring on a clear day. The steep slopes also play host to a gruelling annual

1 Barra, Castlebay **2** Barra, Castle Kisimul **3** Barra, taking off from the cockle strand
4 Barra, machair at Halaman Bay **5** Barra, Our Lady of the Sea

hill race where competitors are free to take any route up and down.

Take a boat to the castle

If arriving at Castlebay by ferry, Kisimul Castle is the first thing to catch your eye as the boat approaches the island. Perched on a tiny rocky skerry in the middle of the bay it couldn't have a better strategic position. A visit starts with a short boat trip before you step ashore to explore the stronghold of the chief of the MacNeil clan who ruled Barra. Built in the 1400s the castle has been restored and includes an impressive feasting hall, chapel and watchman's house. Don't miss the climb to the top of the three-storey tower for a unique view of Castlebay, backed by the steep slopes of Heaval.

Complete the Barrathon

Barra's half marathon takes place each June or July and follows the main road around the island which conveniently clocks in at exactly half-marathon distance. Heading clockwise from Castlebay, the runners are soon heading uphill on a course that quickly weeds out the serious club runners from the so-called 'fun' runners. The mix of undulating course and unpredictable, often windy weather means completing this run earns the respect of anyone on the Scottish running scene. Remember to keep enough stamina for the legendary amounts of fine homebaking provided by the locals, not to mention the post-race ceilidh which has been known to go on well into the wee hours.

Spice up the seafood at Cafe Kisimul

Named for the castle it overlooks, this tiny cafe-cum-bistro on Castlebay's main street packs a hefty punch. Indian and Italian food is given a Barra-style makeover with the emphasis on incorporating as much local fish and seafood as possible. Check out the scallop pakoras or Barra lamb balti. *www.cafekisimul.co.uk*

Cycle the roller-coaster road

The circuit of the island by bike makes for a perfect day out on two wheels. It may be short but be warned – there are very few flat sections! If time allows, detour to the most northerly point passing the beachside airport at Tràigh Mhòr on the way. Compton Mackenzie – the author of *Whisky Galore* and *The Monarch of the Glen* – was a devoted islandphile. He lived for some time on Barra and campaigned to try and ensure the island economy and community was sustainable for the future. Stop off at the tranquil Eoligarry cemetery overlooking the Eriskay ferry jetty to pay your respects. Detouring south to explore the fabulous beaches on Vatersay is also worthwhile if you have anything left in your legs. Bike hire is available in Castlebay.

Make a landing on the cockle strand

While cruising past Kisimul Castle on the CalMac ferry is a pretty dramatic arrival, nothing can beat the adrenaline rush produced from a landing on the beach runway that serves as Barra's airport. Flight times are dependent on the tide and warning flags show the area that whelk collectors, tourists and seaweed-browsing sheep need to keep clear of. The terminal building may well be one of the least stressful airports in the world – going airside means walking round the back, and to approach the plane simply stroll over the beach. The cafe here is open to all.

Picnic on Barra-dise beach

There's no shortage of stunning sandy beaches on Barra but Halaman Bay may just come top of the pile. Located near Tangasdale on the west coast of the island it is backed by flowering machair and dunes. Bike or bus the three kilometres from Castlebay, or take a longer hike around the coast to the site of an ancient fort at Dun Ban before returning to watch the waves from the pristine sands.

Vatersay

Linked to Barra by a 200-metre causeway opened in 1991, Vatersay lays claim to being both the most southerly inhabited island in the Outer Hebrides and the most westerly inhabited place in Scotland. Almost divided in two, the island narrows to a dune and sandy beach-lined isthmus; the community hall serves as a popular cafe here in the summer months. Most people live in the south of the island in Vatersay village which boasts a tiny post office.

Discover the Vatersay Raiders

In 1908 a group of men from Barra and Mingulay were imprisoned following a high-profile court case held in Edinburgh. Their crime had been to seize small areas of land and build huts on Vatersay to try and scratch a living, having been impoverished by overcrowded conditions, disease and the effect of absentee landlords using the island as a source of income. These were cottars who held no land of their own and were therefore at the bottom of the pile. The public sympathy aroused allowed the raiders to continue living on Vatersay on their release. Seek out the ruins of their houses at Eorisdale on a walk around the southern half of the island.

Beware the Vatersay Boys

Hailing from Vatersay and Barra and with two great-grandsons of the Vatersay Raiders in the five-piece line-up, the Vatersay Boys are an energetic band that has taken the traditional Celtic music scene by storm. Despite playing sell-out tours and festivals they can still often be found playing at the Castlebay Bar on Barra, or at Vatersay hall's regular summer weekend ceilidhs. Featuring accordions, pipes, guitar, whistles and driving drums, this is real local music to dance and stomp your feet to.

Fuday

This small island sits between Barra and Eriskay. Now uninhabited, there is evidence of early Norse settlement and records show that before 1901 it supported up to seven people. The island is currently used for summer grazing; traditionally cattle swam the mile-wide strait from Barra. It is said that the first herd of cattle to be put to the summer pasture died of dehydration as they had not been led to the only freshwater source on the island, an inland lochan, and despite the island being only 232 hectares they failed to locate it. Fuday boasts a couple of sandy beaches, one backed by dunes, and a tiny hilltop eighty-nine metres above the sea.

Bishop's Isles (Barra)

The five main islands lying south-east and south of Barra are known as the Bishop's Isles and comprise Maol Dòmhnaich, Sandray, Pabbay, Mingulay and Berneray. They are prized for their birdlife and are gaining popularity with hill baggers (there are several Marilyns) and those seeking a connection with the people who used to inhabit the islands. There are a number of boat operators on Barra who will organise bespoke trips – it is possible to land on all five on a single calm, summer's day, but they also lend themselves to self-sufficient camping stays or day trips.

South of Vatersay, Sandray (Sanndraigh) is a small rocky island boasting cliffs, sea caves and sandy beaches. The last residents left in 1934 and it is now home to a large seabird population. Kayakers can land on one of two sandy beaches.

Together with its southern neighbours Mingulay and Berneray, uninhabited Pabbay (Pabaigh) was bought by the National Trust for Scotland in 2000. The island was evacuated in 1912 after a storm had drowned half the ten-strong male population during a fishing trip in 1897. A bucket-list destination for serious climbers, the cliffs of Lewisian gneiss are regarded as amongst the very best sea cliff climbing venues in Britain. The beautiful and challenging Great Arch includes the fabulously named routes Prophecy of Drowning and Child of the Sea. The first ascents here were by a team that included Chris Bonington and Mick Fowler in 1993. There are only a couple of safe landing sites on Pabbay, which is separated from its immediate neighbours by dangerous tidal flows; a couple of operators on Barra offer boat charter.

Mingulay (Miùghlaigh) attracts the most visitors, a mix of naturalists, hill and island baggers and climbers, but it still remains a lonely and difficult place to reach. A couple of boat operators from Barra are licensed to land on the NTS-owned island but the weather means trips often have to be cancelled at the last minute. The remains of the settlements and burial ground, impressive sea stacks and cliffs teeming with seabirds, rare fauna, and a real sense of isolation make a trip to Mingulay memorable. The island has been uninhabited since it was evacuated at the islanders' request in 1912. Climb to the summit of Carnan at 273 metres for a 360-degree view of the island and neighbouring Berneray.

Also known as Barra Head, Berneray is an exposed island with huge sea cliffs and is the most southerly of the entire Outer Hebridean chain. Most visitors will want to bag the island by climbing to the dramatic clifftop high point of Sotan. A remote community made a living from fishing and crofting until the start of the twentieth century, when only the lighthouse keepers remained. They too left when the Stevenson lighthouse at the far west of the island was fully automated in 1980. If visiting the lighthouse check out the poignant keepers' graveyard nearby. It includes the grave of a two-year-old who died of croup and also a lighthouse inspector who died while visiting the island.

Just off Scotland's north coast, the Orkney archipelago is an archaeological wonderland. This extensive group of islands enjoys a relatively mild climate and fertile soils which have attracted inhabitants for more than 8,500 years. Nowhere in Britain is richer in ancient remains, which include Skara Brae, the best-preserved Neolithic settlement in all Europe, the spectacular Bronze Age tomb of Maes Howe and the stunning standing stones of the Ring of Brodgar. The capital Kirkwall is a vibrant and charming small town, while the outlying islands include Hoy – famed for its Old Man – and a string of lesser-known islands, all with their own secrets to discover.

ORKNEY

Opposite Mainland, Ring of Brodgar   **Overleaf** Westray, Mae Sands

Mainland

The largest island in Orkney is known simply as Mainland. Centrally situated, it is also the hub for transport and services throughout these islands. With an area of 523 square kilometres and an irregular shape with a number of large bays and indented sea lochs, it can take time to really explore Mainland.

Kirkwall is the administrative capital. It has an abundance of historic streets as well as modern services and ferries to many of the northern islands. The island's airport is a short distance to the east. Many visitors arrive in the southern hub of Stromness where the *Hamnavoe*, the large roll-on roll-off ferry from Scrabster near Thurso on the Scottish mainland, lands. Being fairly close to many prehistoric sites, Stromness also makes a good base from which to explore the island. The bus service is relatively good, so with a bit of pre-planning and plenty of time it is possible to bag the island using public transport. If visiting with a bike, bear in mind that Orkney as a whole can be very windy and pedalling into a headwind requires stamina. Mainland, Lamb Holm, Burray and South Ronaldsay are linked by causeways – the latter is served by a vehicle ferry to Gills Bay near John o'Groats.

Descend into Wideford Hill cairn

Some of the most memorable prehistoric sites are those that you can just stumble across with no swish visitor centre or latte-hawking cafe. One of the best on Orkney is within walking distance of Kirkwall. Starting from the Pickaquoy Centre follow Muddisdale Road and then a path to climb Wideford Hill. Fine though the view from the summit is, the real objective lies part way down the far side. Here a sliding trapdoor leads to a ladder accessing a large burial cairn dating back to 3000 BC. You can use the torch provided to explore the interior, where ancient Orcadian farmers were once laid to rest.

Never busy, it's likely you'll have the cairn to yourself so you can practise your Neil Oliver or Alice Roberts impressions in peace.

Take the tour at St Magnus Cathedral

Known as the 'Light in the North', this beautiful red sandstone cathedral was founded in 1137. Dedicated to St Magnus, who was martyred on the island of Egilsay, this great building takes your breath away as you enter and glance upwards to the high vaulted ceiling. To get up there and discover the small, high-level walkways, the clock mechanism and the huge bells, you'll need to book on to one of the tours that run two days a week. Squeeze up the narrow spiral stone staircase, creep along the upper levels and see the cathedral interior in a whole new light. Don't forget to climb the tower for a bird's-eye view of Kirkwall.

Witness the Ba'

Twice a year the narrow streets of Kirkwall's old town are transformed into a heaving mass of players as the 'Uppies' from the top of the town struggle with the 'Doonies' for control of the ball. The huge scrum can number 350 people with games sometimes lasting several hours. The Doonies' goal is the sea of Kirkwall Bay and the Uppies must round the Lang corner where the old town gates used to be. Played on Christmas and New Year's days, the 'no rules' game is strictly for Orcadians but makes a great spectacle for visitors.

Try a beremeal bannock

Bere is an ancient form of barley which was once the main crop on the island, able to withstand the cool climate and short growing season. It's now rare but Barony Mill near Birsay still grinds bere and you can buy a bag of the flour to try making your own bannock. Once a staple for Orcadians, the bannock is a tasty, thick flatbread traditionally cooked on a flat metal griddle over an open fire. Due to the low summer daylight,

climate and poor soil, beremeal has always been a low yielding crop and gave rise to the phrase 'beremeal marriage' – a marriage that would not bring any wealth with it.

Experience the Ring of Brodgar

While we tend to think of Orkney as wild and remote, archaeologists have long argued that it may once have been the epicentre of life in Britain – *the* place to be in Neolithic times. Nowhere is this more apparent than the Ness of Brodgar. Home to Scotland's largest stone circle, walking around the twenty-seven stones which are still standing is an experience not to be missed. When built around 5,000 years ago there were around sixty stones.

Towards Stenness a large area has been a hive of archaeological activity in the summer months for many years, and the dig has so far revealed the remains of numerous buildings including a Neolithic temple. There is evidence that before the complex was closed down around 2200 BC, the ceremonial slaughter of over 400 head of cattle and a huge feast were held, the purpose of which remain a mystery. Equally mysterious are the enormous Stones of Stenness just along the road, where four great monoliths tower over six metres high and were once part of another large stone circle. A sense of great antiquity doesn't get any more palpable than here.

Check out the fitted furniture at the 5,000-year-old houses at Skara Brae

One of the best-preserved Neolithic sites in Europe, Skara Brae was a bustling village well before Stonehenge was built. A huge storm in 1850 uncovered some of the coastal remains and today you can explore nine houses, incredibly some of them still with their stone-built box beds, shelves and furniture. The visitor centre includes a full replica house as well as the obligatory audio-visual presentation, helping to make sense of what you can see on the ground. The setting immediately above the beach adds to the magic. Entry to the nearby seventeenth-century mansion Skaill House is included in the Skara Brae entrance charge.

Walk the west side

This challenging thirty-one-kilometre hike along Mainland's west coast takes in a wealth of stunning scenery, historic sites and wildlife-watching spots. It can be split into sections, or the very fit could hike the lot on a long summer's day. Starting from Stromness the route soon leaves civilisation behind as it rounds the southern tip of Mainland and climbs to the great cliffs of the west coast. The route passes an array of sea stacks including the dramatic two-legged Yesnaby Castle, popular with climbers. Further north it takes in an ancient broch and descends to the Neolithic village of Skara Brae. The next section climbs again along fabulous clifftops to reach the Kitchener Memorial. The tower commemorates the 588 men, including Lord Kitchener, who lost their lives when the HMS *Hampshire* hit a mine and sank just offshore here in 1916. The walk finishes at the imposing ruins of the Earl's Palace in Birsay.

Decipher the Viking graffiti at Maeshowe

Access to Maeshowe, the largest and most mysterious Neolithic tomb on Orkney, is understandably restricted to tours which must be booked in advance. At the appointed time you'll find yourself in a small group, crouched almost on all fours as you negotiate the eleven-

---

metre-long entrance tunnel, the sides of which are, incredibly, single massive slabs. Once the heart of the tomb is reached you can stand comfortably and the exquisite craftsmanship of the people who built the tomb becomes immediately apparent. Flagstones taper inwards forming the beehive-shaped roof of the large central chamber, built over 5,000 years ago. The tomb was discovered and raided by Vikings who left their own marks in the form of runic graffiti. After much painstaking work, historians have managed to translate these thirty early messages, including the highest one which merely boasts that Tholfir Kolbeinsson carved these runes high up – it seems human nature never changes!

Dive into Scapa Flow

Following the First World War armistice the German fleet was held at Scapa Flow while the fate of the ships was negotiated. Fearing the loss of the ships and honour, the German commander ordered the ships to be scuttled in June 1919. Over fifty ships were sunk in the Flow and although many were later salvaged for scrap, a number remain and have become popular dive sites. A number of dive boats operate in the Flow, including two with dive shops in Stromness. One of them offers a half-day dive for complete beginners.

If diving doesn't rock your boat or you need to warm up after a dip in the cold waters of the Flow, a dram of Scapa whisky may be just the tipple. Distilled on the shores of the Flow, Scapa is one of two distilleries on Mainland Orkney, the other being Highland Park.

Follow the ancient path on to the Brough of Deerness

The Brough of Deerness is a massive lump of rocky ground detached from the rest of the Deerness peninsula and jutting out into the North Sea. With thirty-metre vertical cliffs on all sides, getting to the top is a bit of a challenge. First you must descend steep steps into Little Burrageo and then climb the narrow, sloping path to the top. Here are the remains of a settlement which once surrounded a tenth-century chapel, although recent excavations have suggested the ruins are from the Viking era. It's worth continuing around the coast along the high cliffs to Mull Head; the area is a nature reserve.

Step out to an Orcadian Strip the Willow

The traditional music scene is alive and fiddling across Orkney and the best way to experience it is to join a local ceilidh. These can range from semi-formal concerts with a variety of musicians, to dances with a traditional band and a break for homebaking and the ubiquitous raffle. Check out community noticeboards for venues. One of the simplest but most popular ceilidh dances has to be Orcadian Strip the Willow where two lines of men and women face each other and the top couple 'strip' the willow by dancing with their partner alternately with everyone else in the line. If dancing isn't your thing, try and catch a music session at The Reel next to St Magnus Cathedral in Kirkwall where some of the best Orcadian musicians play.

1 Mainland, Maes Howe   **2** Mainland, path on Brough of Deerness   **3** Mainland, Brough of Deerness
4 Mainland, Stromness   **5** Mainland, Mull Head

Brough of Birsay

This tidal island is a must not just for island baggers but for anyone with a taste for history or a love of puffins. Situated at the far north-west of Mainland, the causeway across is only exposed for a couple of hours either side of low tide, so visits need to be planned carefully.

Cross to the Brough

From Point of Buckquoy it's fun to cross the concrete walkway that appears to float over the receding waters of the Sound of Birsay to reach this uninhabited island. Evidence of previous residents is soon on show as the round-island walk passes the remains of a Norse settlement and twelfth-century church. The island's lighthouse is only 11 metres tall, taking advantage of its position perched on the cliffs of Brough Head. These cliffs are also home to numerous seabirds including puffins in the summer. It's possible to make a complete circuit of the cliffs, hopefully with plenty of time to beat the incoming tide.

Lamb Holm

Linked from Mainland Orkney by the first Churchill Barrier – the second and third provide the onward road link to tiny Glimps Holm and then Burray – Lamb Holm is a small uninhabited island that most visitors would whizz across unnoticed were it not for the lasting legacy of Second World War POW Camp 60.

Marvel at the Italian Chapel

Over 500 Italian prisoners of war were housed at Camp 60 on Lamb Holm and used as labour for building the causeways linking the islands and preventing sea access to Scapa Flow. Having been captured in North Africa and transported to Orkney the climate must have been quite a shock to these men. To assist with camp order and morale, the POWs were allowed to transform two Nissen huts into a chapel. Using concrete and plaster, the beautifully ornate facade and interior, including painted frescoes and carvings, were crafted under the direction of Domenico Chiocchetti, who returned twice to Orkney after the war. Today the chapel operates as a poignant visitor attraction.

Burray

Lying between Mainland Orkney and South Ronaldsay, life on Burray changed forever when the causeways were built towards the end of the Second World War, ending the isolation of these southern islands. Burray Village has a shop, school and hotel, and the island has a fascinating museum housing a large fossil collection. Burray is home to around 350 people.

Cross the Churchill Barriers

Home to the British naval fleet during much the Second World War, Scapa Flow had to be heavily defended. The main entrances to this huge natural harbour were obstructed by sunken blockships, anti-submarine nets and mines, all backed up by land-based lookouts and artillery. Despite these efforts, a German U-boat slunk into the Flow just north of Burray

1 Brough of Birsay, kirk ruins **2** Brough of Birsay, causeway **3** Lamb Holm, Churchill Barrier
4 and **5** Lamb Holm, Italian chapel

during high tide in October 1939. It sunk HMS *Royal Oak* with the loss of 833 men. Following these terrible losses Winston Churchill ordered the construction of permanent barriers.

The barriers were built primarily by 1,200 prisoners of war based in camps on Burray and Lamb Holm. The use of POWs for war work is prohibited by the Geneva Conventions but the British have always argued that the work was for improving communications and certainly that has been the benefit for modern-day Orcadians. There are four barriers, the first linking Mainland Orkney with Lamb Holm, the next links to Glimps Holm, then Burray, and finally Barrier 4 continues to South Ronaldsay. Cross them all and you will also see some of the original blockships projecting from the water.

Hunda

Constructed during the Second World War, possibly as a practice run for the Churchill Barriers built to block German U-boat access to the British naval fleet, the causeway to Hunda means it's easy to access this delightful small island. A mere 100 hectares in size, the island is uninhabited and currently used for sheep grazing – its name comes from the Norse for 'dog island'.

Cross the causeway to Hunda

The 500-metre-long stone and concrete causeway offers a grand approach to Hunda. The island itself is easily walked around in half a day – there is a clear path, excellent views, plenty of birdlife and the chance to spot otters, seals and passing porpoises. There's no parking at Littlequoy so it's best to walk in along the track from Burray Village, eventually making for the coast before the crossing of the causeway at Hunda Reef.

South Ronaldsay

South Ronaldsay is the fourth largest of the Orkney islands with just under 5,000 hectares of relatively fertile land. It is surrounded by a hugely indented coastline boasting a variety of cliffs, arches and caves, and sandy beaches. The large vehicle ferry, the *Pentalina*, is a catamaran and runs from Gills Bay on the Scottish mainland to St Margaret's Hope, while the John o'Groats passenger ferry disgorges a large number of visitors on to coach tours as well as cyclists and others at Burwick at the southern end of the island. Most services are found in St Margaret's Hope, although there are eating and accommodation options throughout the island.

Get off your trolley in the Tomb of the Eagles

Numerous well-preserved Neolithic tombs are dotted around Orkney, but this is the only one usually entered by lying on your back – visitors haul themselves through the entrance on a small, wheeled trolley, though knee pads are provided for those who prefer to crawl! Once inside, this coastal cairn reveals several chambers including one where farmer Ronnie Simison discovered 30 human skulls after stumbling across the site in 1958. Still in family hands, the cairn and museum are surprisingly hands-on with visitors encouraged to handle some of the finds and chat to Ronnie's two enthusiastic and knowledgeable daughters. The tomb is named after the large number of eagle talons discovered during the excavations; it is likely that the birds had a symbolic significance for the people who lived and were buried here 5,000 years ago.

Clear your head at Hoxa

Hoxa Head is one of the best places to explore wartime defences and get a feeling for how central Orkney was for Britain's naval fleet during both world wars. From a small parking area a path leads around to Hoxa Head, offering great views over the spectacular natural harbour that is Scapa Flow. Along the way you'll find the remains of a large number of gun batteries, bunkers and a small lighthouse used to defend the narrow Sound of Hoxa that lies

between here and the island of Flotta. Huge underwater nets, as well as mines activated from the shore, were hung across to Stanger Head on Flotta to try and prevent German U-boats accessing the anchorage during both world wars. Now home to grazing sheep and seabirds, it is worth continuing around the coast to pass three deep inlets – known as geos – in the cliffs before returning past the site of a military camp to the start of the walk near The Bu.

Hike the east coast

This challenging half-day walk is the best opportunity to get a real taste for South Ronaldsay's coastline: a mix of low and high cliffs, many with impressive flagstone strata; deep sea inlets or geos; and a gloup, a collapsed cave which now acts as a blowhole in stormy weather. Start from Burwick near the pier for the John o'Groats ferry and head south initially to round Brough Ness before the coast curves to the north. The walk diverts inland to pass the visitor centre for the Tomb of the Eagles chambered cairn, and the tomb itself is passed another 1.5 kilometres further along the coast. Look out for peregrine falcons at Mouster Head before the walk reaches its final stage crossing the wide sandy arc of Newark Bay to reach one of Orkney's oldest parish churches, St Peter's Kirk. From here you would need to have arranged transport or it's a three-kilometre walk on quiet roads to St Margaret's Hope.

Hoy

Hoy is the second largest of the Orkney islands, and its name comes from the Norse word *haey* meaning 'high' – a reference to Hoy's great hills and cliffs. A car ferry from Houton on Orkney Mainland links to Lyness at the southern end of Hoy, or to Longhope on neighbouring South Walls which is linked by a causeway. There's also a useful passenger ferry service from Stromness which lands at Moaness in north Hoy (usually via Graemsay).

Most facilities and shops are found in the south of the island including hotel, pub and bed and breakfast accommodation. There is a cafe and hostel at Moaness and another tiny hostel at Rackwick.

Visit the Old Man of Hoy

First climbed in 1966, this iconic pillar of red sandstone is a must-see for every visitor to Hoy. None of the climbing routes on this 137-metre sea stack are graded less than Extremely Severe, and reaching the base involves a potentially dangerous rope traverse. But even if you'll never get up there to add your name to the logbook stored in a box in the summit cairn, reaching the clifftops opposite on Hoy's dramatic coast is good enough for most island baggers. The shortest approach is from Rackwick Bay, just over a nine-kilometre round trip on a clear track and path. If you don't have a car on Hoy then you can walk from Moaness to Rackwick through the Rackwick Glen, another seven kilometres each way.

Squeeze inside the Dwarfie Stane

It's not often you get to crawl *inside* a prehistoric carved boulder. The Dwarfie Stane, a Neolithic rock-cut tomb, can be found not far from the road to Rackwick in the glaciated valley below Ward Hill. Hollowed out from a single block of stone using primitive tools before metal had been discovered, the entrance leads to two side chambers, each just long enough to hold a body (or two) and featuring a rougher 'pillow'. The original stone slab which sealed the entrance sits on the ground outside. Local legend suggests a giant and his wife originally lived in the Stane and were imprisoned in it by a third giant who wanted to rule Hoy. The captors are said to have gnawed their way out through the roof, neatly explaining the hole which is presumed to have been made by grave robbers and has been there since the sixteenth century.

Experience a bonxie bombing

Hoy is home to the second largest colony of great skuas in Britain. Known locally as bonxies, these large birds have a grace and speed of movement in the air, lacking when on the ground. These 'pirates of the sea' harry other seabirds until they drop their catch, at which point the skuas help themselves to the still-warm takeaway. They will also take eggs and young chicks from nests in cliffs, as well as dive-bomb unsuspecting walkers who get too close to this ground-nesting bird during the breeding season. The best place to see them on Hoy is on the wide plateau of Cuilags, most easily accessed via the ridge facing the Moaness Pier ferry. Hillwalkers with the energy and time can extend the walk over the Sui Fea plateau before heading to the immense cliffs of St John's Head. The coastal cliffs can then be followed southwards to the Old Man of Hoy and on to Rackwick Bay.

1 Hoy, Scad Head **2 Hoy,** the Old Man of Hoy

Discover Orkney's native woodland

Lying deep in Rackwick Glen, Berriedale Wood is thought to be a remnant of the type of woodland that would have covered most of Orkney and Shetland around 7,000 years ago. Today it is an important habitat for other wildlife making a home amongst its downy birch, hazel, rowan, aspen, willow and roses. Find it nestled in a deep gully on the west side of Rackwick Glen about two and half kilometres from Rackwick. Those keen to spot more wildlife should keep their eyes peeled for white-tailed eagles – a pair has nested on crags above the Dwarfie Stane and successfully hatched a chick for the first time in 2018. The sheer size of these birds, with a wing span of well over two metres, makes them hard to miss.

Survey all Orkney from Ward Hill

It is said that from the summit of Ward Hill, the highest point on Hoy and indeed all Orkney, all the islands except one – Rysa Little – can be seen. You'd certainly need to be blessed with good weather, but the ascent is worth it for the views of Scapa Flow and Hoy alone. All ascent routes are very steep. One option is to head up from the road near the Dwarfie Stane – your calf muscles will be screaming on the unrelenting turf-clutching ascent. The summit of Haist (333 metres) is visited en route to the main summit of Ward Hill, the highest point in Orkney at 479 metres. It is possible to descend to the bealach between it and Cuilags before returning past Sandy Loch.

Search for the searchlights at Scad Head

No trip to Hoy is complete without visiting some of the sites associated with the island's prominent role in the Second World War.

Over 12,000 military personnel were stationed on Hoy during the war, mostly at Lyness, dwarfing the island's small population. The Scapa Flow Visitor Centre is a great place to learn more and explore the remaining building which includes the Navy, Army and Air Force Institutes (NAAFI) recreation centre where over 1,900 used the cinema, dance hall and leisure facilities a week. There are also air raid shelters and a naval cemetery. The most atmospheric place to contrast the beautiful peacetime landscape with the wartime reality is at Scad Head. Here the remains of coastal gun emplacements and lookout towers contrast oddly with their surroundings. It's now simply a surreal place from which to watch the seabirds and seals. Halfway between Lyness and Quoyness, the remains of an old tramway lead down to Scad Head – if time allows you can make a circuit by walking up to the viewpoint on Lyrawa Hill.

South Walls

South Walls is attached by a causeway known as the Ayre to the south-east corner of Hoy. Originally a tidal island, the causeway made access more permanent during the First World War. The island shelters the North Bay and includes the settlement of Longhope where the ferry from Houton and Flotta calls, alternating with stops at Lyness on Hoy.

Climb the Martello Tower at Hackness

The robust circular Martello Tower at the Point of Hackness is one of a pair guarding the Switha Sound between South Walls and Flotta. Built during the Napoleonic Wars to protect a northern trade route to Scandinavia and Baltic

---

1 Hoy, Berriedale Wood **2** Hoy, Dwarfie Stane **3** Hoy, Ward Hill **4** Hoy, battery at Scad Head **5** Hoy, view from Ward Hill

ports from French and American attacks, it never saw action. Today you can climb the ladder to the high entrance door and imagine what life was like for those stationed at this remote fortress. Open April to the end of September, the tower is operated by Historic Environment Scotland and there is an entrance charge.

Light your candle on the amazing south coast

The south coast of South Walls boasts an embarrassment of natural sea features. Arches, caves, blowholes and stacks all vie for your attention on the seven-kilometre walk between the Ayre and Cantick Head. Keep a particular eye out for the Axe and the Candle, both prominent sea stacks. The cliffs are home to numerous seabirds and the keen-eyed may spot peregrine falcons as well as Arctic skuas hunting amongst the nesting birds. Look beneath your feet and you might see a purple Scottish primrose which flowers in May and August. The walk finishes with a dramatic approach to Cantick Head lighthouse. It is possible to make a circuit by returning inland to the Ayre via Osmondwall.

Graemsay

Graemsay, a fertile island known as 'Orkney's Green Isle', has a population of around twenty-five.

The passenger ferry to Hoy from Stromness stops at Graemsay and takes only fifteen minutes when going direct, though it often calls first at Hoy, extending the journey time to forty-five minutes. Expect to share the journey with schoolchildren and commuters from both islands.

Highlights and low lights

The best way to see the island is on foot and it's easy to walk all the way round the island in a day between ferries. Once on Graemsay follow the road towards Hoy High Lighthouse; one of a pair of Stevenson lighthouses on the island, this one is thirty-three metres tall. Continuing on the road, the verge often ablaze with orchids and other wild flowers, pass the community hall and descend to the coast. Rougher walking hugs the coastline, passing the Low Lighthouse (a mere twelve metres tall), a Second World War gun battery. On the foreshore you may find pottery fragments from an 1866 shipwreck which claimed the lives of eleven people. It's necessary to return to the road for a distance before a final stretch along the south coast offers great views of Hoy. After passing the remote Old Kirk the route returns to the ferry pier having completed a 360-degree tour of the island.

Flotta

Flotta lies at the southern end of Scapa Flow and has a resident population of around eighty, although many more people commute to the island every day to work at the large oil terminal which handles around ten per cent of the UK's oil. The island also experienced two huge but temporary population explosions during the two world wars. Ferries to Flotta run from Houton on Orkney Mainland, and also from Lyness on Hoy and Longhope on South Walls.

See the sea stacks

Sometimes overlooked as a place to visit because of the industrial oil terminal, the rest of Flotta is very quiet and green, with good views over Scapa Flow and to Hoy. However,

1 South Walls, coast walk   **2** South Walls, Hackness martello tower   **3** Graemsay, Hoy High lighthouse
4 Flotta, sculptures   **5** Flotta, the ferry   **6** Flotta, battery overlooking Scapa Flow   **7** Flotta, stacks at Stanger Head

184

the highlight has to be Flotta's sea stacks, closely followed by the quirky scrap metal sculptures dotted about the island. Both can be seen from the fifteen-kilometre trail around the southern half of the island. The cletts, or sea stacks, make for an impressive view from Stanger Head, and both are wider at the top than the bottom. While on the trail see how many of the Flotta-made recycled sculptures you can spot – the three penguins are a favourite.

Rousay

Rousay is a must for any island bagger, offering an amazing range of archaeological sites outside the mainstream tourism circuit of Mainland. This small, hilly island is one of great character, deserving a full exploration. The car ferry runs from Tingwall on Mainland – but be warned if you are taking a vehicle you will have to reverse either on or off. The same ferry also links Egilsay and Wyre to Mainland. Rousay has a primary school and a cafe/pub, and is home to just over 200 people.

Dig in to Rousay's deep past
A short walk along the coast at Westside leads through thousands of years of history. First up is Midhowe Cairn – a huge chambered burial cairn where human remains were placed in separate stalls within the 4,000-year-old structure. Today a modern building protects the old one from the elements, so that the latter remains as well preserved as when it was first excavated in 1932. Just along the coast is a large and well-preserved Iron Age broch, perched on the water's edge. You can still see the double-wall construction of this defensive building. For a chance to watch modern-day time-teamers in action, head back along the coast, passing the

sixteenth-century St Mary's Kirk, to reach the site of the archaeological dig at Swandro. Every summer archaeologists and students descend on the site keen to uncover the secrets of the Pictish and Viking buildings before storms and rising sea levels take their toll.

Top out on Blotchnie Fiold
The highest point on Rousay is part of an RSPB reserve, famed for its birds of prey including short-eared owls. The seven-and-a-half-kilometre round trip can easily be done in half a day, leaving plenty of time to clamber inside the 5,000-year-old Taversoe Tuick chambered burial cairn passed on the way up from the ferry pier. The route climbs over heather moorland, following old peat cuttings for a time; it has occasional waymarkers. Climb to the high point of Blotchnie Fiold (250 metres) before another climb to reach the trig point on the lower summit of Knitchen Hill. From here the view is all expansive skies, and the blue sea dotted with green isles. If time allows there is a fascinating heritage centre near the ferry and also a cafe/bar.

Take a Rousay Lap
The undulating road around Rousay is 13.1 miles long, lending itself to the annual half marathon – the Rousay Lap – which takes place in August. Steep in places with two notable hills known locally as the Leeon and Sourin Brae, it's incredibly scenic. Free to enter, the event is open to cyclists, runners and walkers, and if it's all too much there's also a five-kilometre Peedie Lap each June. Even if you can't take part on the day, the road round Rousay makes for a great half-day cycle ride. A number of detours on foot enable you to visit the brochs and cairns for which the island is famous, and the gardens at Trumland House are also worth a visit. Cycle hire is available from Trumland Organic Farm.

1 Rousay, on Blotchnie Fiold   **2 Rousay**, ferry jetty   **3 Rousay**, the ferry, Eynhallow
4 Rousay, Taversoe Tuick chambered cairn   **5 Rousay**, broch   **6 Rousay**, path on Knitchen Hill

Egilsay

Linked by ferry from Tingwall on Mainland via either Rousay or Wyre, Egilsay is a long thin island with a resident population of around fifteen. Home to the elusive corncrake in the summer, it's a good place for a quiet wildlife wander or a natter with friendly locals. Its size makes it ideal for a half day's exploration on foot or by bike. The community hall is open to visitors with an honesty system for hot drinks.

Watch your head at St Magnus Church

The distinctive cylindrical tower of St Magnus Church is unmissable as the ferry draws into Egilsay. An ancient place of pilgrimage, it was here that Magnus was killed by an axe blow to the head. Having shared the Viking kingdom in an uneasy alliance with Earl Haakon, the two rulers arranged a meeting on Egilsay in 1115. On arrival it was obvious that Haakon intended to kill him, having arrived with boatloads of armed men. Magnus led his men to pray in the church, and he was duly executed. Although it featured in the *Orkneyinga Saga*, what seems like the stuff of legend became more real when a skull with a large crack in it – possibly caused by an axe – was discovered in the walls of St Magnus Cathedral in Kirkwall.

Wyre

The smallest of the three islands linked by ferry from Tingwall on Mainland, Wyre is reached either via Rousay or Egilsay. Known for the seals

1 Egilsay, isolated farmstead   **2 Wyre,** Cubbie Roo's castle   **3 Egilsay,** St Magnus Church

which haul out at The Taing at the westernmost point on the island, Wyre also has a heritage centre packed full of fascinating photographs and information about life on the island.

Check out Cubbie Roo's Castle

Cubbie Roo was a man so massive that according to legend he used many of Orkney's islands as stepping stones. He is said to have made Wyre his home, and the castle built around 1145 is one of the oldest castles in all Scotland. Most of the stories surrounding Cubbie Roo have him trying to build stone bridges between islands or hurling boulders across the water to their current resting places. One tells that he built a bridge between Wyre and Rousay that collapsed and formed the mound known as Cubbie Roo's Burden. The castle remains can be found next to the twelfth-century ruins of St Mary's Chapel – turn right off the main road just before the heritage centre on the way from the ferry.

Westray

The sixth largest and one of the more remote major islands in Orkney, fertile Westray lies over thirty-two kilometres north of Kirkwall and is home to around 600 people. It is served by a vehicle ferry which takes an hour and half to reach Rapness, where it is usually met by a bus. There are also daily flights from Kirkwall. Although most shops and services are centred on the main settlement Pierowall, accommodation is scattered across the island, including hotels, bed and breakfasts, self-catering, a hostel and camping. There are two general stores in Pierowall, one of which also has a cafe. Jack's Chippy, also in Pierowall, is a takeaway very popular with locals. There is also a well-stocked general store and post office at Skelwick.

Pootle with the puffins at Castle o'Burrian

Westray is the best place in Orkney to see puffins. Many visitors come here especially to see them, and Castle o'Burrian is the place to do it. The Castle is actually a large sea stack, detached from the cliff and with a thick wodge of turf on top for the puffins to make their burrows safe from predators and the blundering feet of birdwatchers. Take the coast path for approximately one and a half kilometres from Rapness Mill at Rack Wick bay in the south of the island and find a comfortable place to sit opposite the Castle and let the show begin; keep a look out just below the path, as many puffins nest right by it too. These colourful and characterful birds spend most of the year at sea, coming ashore from May to July to breed.

Get a head for heights at   Noup Head

The seventy-six-metre-high cliffs at Noup Head are the best place to see the masses of seabirds that come to Westray to breed during the spring and early summer. The flagstone cliffs have formed millions of natural ledges which are used by gannets, guillemots and kittiwakes, while the springy turf on top provides a home for puffins and Arctic terns. This is a great place to visit at any time of year as the cliffs and nearby natural arches and caves are spectacular, while the now solar-powered Stevenson lighthouse makes a great focal point. The shape and terracing of the cliffs here provided the inspiration to architect Kengo Kuma for his striking V&A building on Dundee's waterfront. There's no public transport but Noup Head is a short cycle ride from Pierowall, or you can drive along the bumpy track to the lighthouse. It's also possible to make a circular walk from Backarass.

Discover the nousts at Mae Sand

Westray's eighty-kilometre coastline boasts eighteen sandy beaches and all are worth discovering. Mae Sand is particularly atmospheric – and usually deserted – and you can still see the shelters once used by Vikings to store their boats. Mae Sand can be approached on foot via a rough coastal path from Tuqouy or via the tiny settlement of Langskaill. Search for the boat-shaped drystane-walled depressions at the back of the beach – these are where early Norse settlers would have protected their boats. Known as 'nousts', they have been used by Westray folk for generations. The recently built Westray skiff bears a striking resemblance to open boats used right back to Viking times.

Nibble on Westray Wife

The Westray Wife is a 5,000-year-old figurine also known as the 'Orkney Venus'. Discovered at the Links of Noltland in 2009, it was the first Neolithic carving of a human figure found in Scotland. Only four centimetres tall, the figure consists of a round 'head' and square 'body'. Find it at the Westray Heritage Centre in Pierowall. To really get a taste for Westray life, sample the moreish washed-rind cheese also known as Westray Wife, produced on the island by Wilsons of Westray and available in local shops.

Papa Westray

This remote island, known locally as Papay, sits to the north-east of Westray and can be visited from there either via the world's shortest scheduled flight, or by passenger ferry from Gill Pier in Pierowall. As well as bed and breakfast and self-catering accommodation, there is a modern hostel at Beltane House close to the community shop. Bicycle hire is available by contacting the Papay ranger (details on Facebook).

Walk the island circuit

Hiking right round the coastline makes for a fantastic day out – take in the high flagstone cliffs, endless sandy beaches, rich farmland and ancient buildings to get a real feel for island life. Start by turning right at Moclett pier and following the coast path past the Bay of Burland. The huge white sands of South Wick offer tantalising views to the tiny Holm of Papa just offshore. Further along, the RSPB North Hill reserve is reached. The cliffs here offer great spots for watching the black guillemots, and further on you may have to defend yourself against aggressive terns who nest on the far side of Mull Head. The west coast of the island is gentler and includes the serene and ancient St Boniface Kirk, and then the impressive and well-preserved Neolithic farmstead the Knap of Howar, said to be the oldest north European dwelling still standing. The circuit of the island finishes by crossing a fine sandy beach, not the worst place to wait for the return ferry.

Find the last great auk

It was on the cliffs of Fowl Craig that the world's last breeding pair of great auk were killed, causing the extinction of the species within thirty years. Also known as the 'northern penguin', these flightless black and white birds stood a metre tall. The male was shot by local man, William Foulis, on the command of a collector in 1813; the female and her egg had been destroyed the previous year. Although excellent swimmers, great auks moved slowly on land and having few natural predators they were not naturally scared of humans. First killed for their meat and feathers, the last birds were

1 **Westray**, Castle o' Burrian   2 **Westray**, sunset at Tuquoy   3 **Westray**, puffin at Castle o'Burrian   4 **Westray**, Mae Sand
5 **Westray**, Noup Head   6 **Westray**, signpost   7 **Papa Westray**, the last great auk   8 **Papa Westray**, North Hill RSPB reserve

shot as specimens for museums and private collections. A small memorial stands on Fowl Craig which today is a great place to spot our surviving species of auks, namely guillemots, razorbills, black guillemots and puffins. Fowl Craig is found on the north-east of the island and can be reached on foot along the coast or by cycling as far as Hundland.

Holm of Papa

The Holm is a small – twenty-one hectares – uninhabited island that sits in South Wick bay just off the east coast of Papa Westray. Known locally as Papay Holm, visits can be arranged by private boat – ask at the Papa Westray community shop. The main attraction is a twenty-metre-long chambered burial cairn known as Southcairn with a characteristically Orcadian stalled structure.

Shapinsay

Shapinsay is a mere twenty-five minutes by ferry from Kirkwall, and as a result many of its 300 or so residents work in Orkney's capital, commuting by sea. This fertile, low-lying island is mainly given over to farming with a couple of small nature reserves known for waterfowl, waders and Arctic terns. The approach to Shapinsay by ferry is dominated by Balfour Castle. This large Scottish Baronial pile dates back to the 1840s and was originally designed as a so-called 'calendar house' comprising fifty-two rooms, twelve exterior doors, seven turrets and 365 panes of glass. It's a private home, but the former gatehouse near the ferry slipway now houses the island pub. There is also a shop, cafe and heritage centre in the small village of Balfour.

Check out the Shapinsay shower

From the harbour it's a short walk south along the coast to reach a prominent stone tower. Originally built as a dovecote used to breed the birds for meat back in the seventeenth century, it was later converted to use as a saltwater shower by David Balfour as part of his works completing the castle in the 1840s. It's not possible to enter the tower – known locally as 'the douche' – but it can be visited by a brief walk from the ferry pier. It's possible to continue round the coast to Vasa Loch before heading back to Balfour on quiet lanes.

Eday

Eday is fourteen kilometres long but narrows to a mere 500 metres at one point, giving rise to its name which comes from the Norse for 'isthmus island'. Today it is linked by daily vehicle ferries from Kirkwall on Mainland which land at Backaland in the south of the island, and by a weekly inter-island flight from Kirkwall. There has been talk of building bridges or causeways to link to nearby Westray. The island has a population of around 160, down from a high of just under a thousand in the early 1800s. There is a heritage centre with cafe, small store, hostel, bed and breakfast and self-catering accommodation, and bike hire.

Journey through time

Eday has a rich array of archaeological sites and the island's heritage trail means you can explore them all on foot. The route starts at the shop – either use the bus from the ferry or bike or walk – and soon passes the four-and-a-half-metre tall Stone of Setter, one of the tallest standing stones in Orkney. Follow marker posts towards Vinquoy Hill, passing two smaller chambered cairns before reaching Vinquoy chambered

cairn, thought to be at least 4,000 years old. The walk then heads past old peat cuttings to reach a trig point on the cliffs at the most northerly point of the island – a wonderful vantage point and a good place to watch the seabirds before the return leg.

Hang out with the seals

Many come to Eday for some peaceful wildlife watching and setting yourself the target of spotting a seal or even an otter or red-throated diver is one way to bag the island. The divers arrive in the summer and can often be seen on Mill Loch where there is a handy hide. If you hear a regular whirring sound it's likely to be a snipe and you can add that to the wildlife tick list. For seals, head to the very south of the island where they often haul out at the Point of War Ness. Keep an eye out here too for passing dolphins, minke whales and the very occasional orca.

Stronsay

Known as the 'Island of Bays' due to its irregular shape indented by three fine beaches, Stronsay is a low-lying island which is home to around 300 people. It is linked to Mainland Orkney via a daily ferry from Kirkwall to Whitehall, sometimes stopping at Eday en route. There are also daily flights on the island hopper from Kirkwall airport. There is a hotel, bed and breakfast, hostel, two cafes, school and two general shops including Ebenezer Stores which also offers free bikes for visitors.

Check out the Vat of Kirbister

Stronsay's standout feature is a collapsed sea cave with an impressive natural arch spanning the entrance to a gloup, or blowhole. It can be visited as part of a twelve-kilometre circular walk that heads around Lamb Head, starting from

1 Shapinsay, the douche   **2 Eday,** Stone of Setter

the parking area near Kirbuster Farm. The huge rock arch itself is soon reached but the rest of the coastline is no disappointment. A couple of high sea stacks include Tam's Castle on which a hermit is said to have lived. Nowadays it's home to a whirling cacophony of fulmars and guillemots. Two more headlands and a number of deep geos keep adding interest to the walk before the final section through farmland leads back to the start.

Search for mermaids at the Sands of Rothiesholm

It's hard to choose a favourite but the Sands of Rothiesholm just pips St Catherine's Bay to the post in the battle to be Stronsay's finest beach. The bright white sands stretch out for over 1,500 metres, and beachcombers can search for the rare woody canoe-bubble shell, a type of sea snail shell found in shades from cream to orangey-brown. Mermaids are even rarer – if you're really desperate to spot one you may need to head over to Mill Bay on the east of the island where they are said to have been seen reclining on the rocks in the middle of the bay. The Sands of Rothiesholm has its own semi-mythical beast – a seventeen-metre-long creature washed ashore in 1808 which was thought to be some kind of unknown sea serpent. Modern commentators suggest it may have been the bloated body of a long-dead basking shark.

Papa Stronsay

Lying just north-east of Stronsay, Papa Stronsay provides shelter for the ferry pier on its parent island. It has long been associated with those of a religious calling, being the site of a seventh- or eighth-century monastery. Today it is home to a congregation of traditional Catholic Redemptorist monks who run the Golgotha Monastery, farm the island and offer residential retreats. If rising for prayers at 5 a.m. isn't your thing it may be possible to arrange a boat trip to the island with the monks.

Sanday

A quick look at an aerial photograph of Sanday reveals vast amounts of sandy beach giving rise to the island's original Norse name of *Sandey*. The third largest of the Orkney islands, Sanday is divided into three peninsulas and is home to over 500 people. The island boasts a couple of shops (including the cavernous Sinclair General Stores where you can pretty much buy anything), a couple of hotels, a hostel, bed and breakfasts, self-catering cottages and even a community-run swimming pool.

Sanday is served by a roll-on roll-off ferry twice a day from Kirkwall on Mainland, often via Eday or Stronsay. There are also daily flights from Kirkwall. An on-demand bus operates on the island and should be booked in advance.

Dodge the tides to reach Start Point

Start Point lighthouse is built on a tidal islet sitting off the most easterly point of Sanday and can only be reached at low tide. Start from the road end beyond Thrave and head over the exposed pebbly causeway of Ayre Sound, aiming for the lighthouse. Vertical black and white stripes give this Stevenson lighthouse a unique appearance. The first Scottish lighthouse to have a revolving light, it replaced a more basic tower which proved inadequate at stopping ships getting wrecked just offshore. The massive stone ball from that tower now sits

1 Stronsay, Sands of Rothiesholm   **2** Stronsay, Vat of Kirbuster

1

2

atop the old lighthouse on North Ronaldsay. Tours of the lighthouse can be arranged with the Sanday ranger. If visiting during the summer take care not to disturb the terns that nest off the foreshore – they will certainly let you know loud and clear if you get too close!

Crawl into Quoyness cairn

A slightly less grand version of Maeshowe, this 5,000-year-old chambered burial chamber is one of the finest you'll find anywhere, enhanced by a fantastic shoreside setting and lack of visitors. The cairn is made more atmospheric by the nine-metre crawl along the low entrance passage before you can stand up in the square central space. A torch is handy for exploring the side chambers. The best approach is to walk from Lady, crossing the narrow strip of Quoy Ayre with the sea either side before following the coast to the cairn.

Beachcomb at Whitemill Bay

The bleached sand of Whitemill Bay is the perfect backdrop for a spot of beachcombing. Starting from the parking area at the western end of the bay, this long arc of sand, backed by dunes, eventually leads to Whitemill Point where seals often haul out at low tide. Even if you have the sands to yourself, continue around the coast to the ruined farmstead at Helliehow and you may find yourself with a Hogboon for company. Rather like an imp, the Hogboon is a mythical figure said to have bullied the farm residents into moving only to hide himself amongst their belongings to continue his persecution of them – Helliehow remains deserted to this day.

Sample crofting life

Step through the low door of The Croft to see how life was lived in the early part of the twentieth century. Restored by locals, this typical two-roomed croft house sits alongside Sanday Heritage Centre on the outskirts of Lady village. Inside are box beds, a peat range complete with griddle for making oatcakes and bannocks, Orkney chairs made the traditional way from driftwood with woven backs, and plenty of genuine household items giving an authentic feel. Chat with the volunteers who helped restore the house; some of them remember growing up in properties just like this one.

North Ronaldsay

North Ronaldsay is an Orcadian anomaly: the most isolated inhabited island in the island group, it is served only twice a week by car ferry (weekly in the winter), though there are daily flights from Kirkwall. A visit here feels like a real step back in time from Orkney's other islands. Although low-lying it is extremely rocky and exposed, and is best known for its seaweed-eating sheep and its two lighthouses. It's home to fewer than seventy people, although there are moves to try and encourage more people to move here. The isolation means it's a popular spot for migratory birds – there's a bird observatory which also provides the main visitor accommodation, cafe and evening meals for guests. There's also a cafe at the lighthouse. As with the other islands, the return flight is cheaper if you stay on the island overnight.

Walk the wall

A twenty-kilometre drystane dyke (wall) has been used since 1832 to keep North Ronaldsay's sheep on the foreshore where

---

1 Sanday, The Croft　**2** Sanday, Start Point lighthouse　**3** Sanday, Whitemill Bay　**4** and **5** Sanday, Quoyness chambered cairn

they graze on the seaweed, freeing up the land inside for cultivation. The complete walk around the wall is an obscure Orkney classic, though it is rough-going in places and a tough undertaking to complete in one go. If you are fit and determined it can make a wonderful day, with plenty of opportunities for a bit of bird or seal watching. The very distinctive, shaggy brown to red Ronaldsay sheep will be your companions. They are smaller than more modern breeds and have adapted to life on the foreshore, grazing at low tide and ruminating at high tide. The gamey-tasting meat is particularly prized and served at a number of restaurants across Orkney. The island hosts an annual Sheep Festival where volunteers help repair the dyke as well as taking part in wool-related activities.

Visit the bird observatory

As Orkney's most northerly island, North Ronaldsay is renowned by twitchers as the place to watch migratory birds in the spring and autumn and spot rare species that are unexpectedly blown in. The bird observatory is the place to hear about recent sightings and other bird-related news. It was founded in 1987 and has monitored the birds visiting the island ever since. Anyone can stay at the observatory which has bed and breakfast, hostel and camping accommodation, as well as a cafe; they often serve North Ronaldsay lamb. The observatory also has a number of opportunities for ornithological volunteers. *www.nrbo.org.uk*

1 and **2 North Ronaldsay,** the lighthouse   **3 North Ronaldsay,** the wall   **4 North Ronaldsay,** Ronaldsay sheep

Visit the light

Head to the north of the island to see the twin lighthouses that have served to protect seafarers from this stretch of coast which is notorious for shipwrecks. The Old Beacon is a twenty-one-metre-tall stone lighthouse built at Dennis Head in 1789 and lit with a series of oil burners and copper reflectors. The light was extinguished in 1809 when the Start Point lighthouse on Sanday came onstream, and the lantern here was replaced by the massive stone ball seen today. A number of wrecks proved the provision at Start Point was inadequate and the red-and-white-striped lighthouse was built just along the coast in 1852. At forty-three metres it is the tallest land-based lighthouse in the whole of the UK. A visitor centre, cafe and self-catering accommodation are housed in the lighthouse buildings.

Copinsay

Copinsay lies to the east of Mainland Orkney and is best seen from the Deerness peninsula. Now uninhabited, it is an RSPB bird reserve and its farmland is managed to foster wildlife including corncrakes. A huge number of seabirds including razorbills, guillemots, fulmars, puffins, black guillemots and shags nest on the high cliffs during the breeding season. The island is also home to a large colony of grey seals who pup here every November. Up until 1958 there was a resident farming population on the island as well as the lighthouse keepers and their families; the latter remained until 1991. Visiting the island relies on private boat charter or kayak but the tidal currents are particularly dangerous so local knowledge should be sought. Adjacent is the Horse of Copinsay, little more than a sea stack but with the attraction of Blaster Hole, a large blowhole, which can be viewed from a passing boat.

Stroma

Lying in the Pentland Firth between Orkney and the Scottish mainland, Stroma belongs to neither. It was home to over 300 people at the beginning of the twentieth century but is now abandoned. The population fell rapidly until the last permanent residents left in 1962, though lighthouse keepers continued to live here until 1997.

The houses in many of the two settlements are still standing – left to a slow decay, in many cases they still have all their furniture inside. The ferocious tides of the Firth that contributed to the decline of the community continue to make access difficult; it may be possible to arrange a charter boat from John o'Groats.

Swona

This smaller island to the north of Stroma suffered a similar fate, though it held on to its last inhabitants – a brother and sister – until 1974. While still in the ownership of two Orkney farms, the island is no longer farmed due to the difficulty of access. When the last people left – one was sick, and the other knew she might not be able to return – the sister released their beef cattle, eight cows and a bull, to roam free on the island. Several generations later the herd is still going strong and numbered seventeen at the last count. Living completely feral, the beasts have reverted to natural behaviour.

Landing on the island is difficult, and the good view of it from the *Pentalina* ferry from Gills Bay to Orkney is as close as most people will get.

Lying over 160 kilometres from Scotland's mainland, Shetland is so far north that on many maps of the UK it appears in its own inset box. Culture here has a distinctly Scandinavian influence, and the community has been greatly strengthened by money from North Sea oil. Reaching Shetland takes a real effort, but the rewards are rich. The islands are particularly renowned for their bird life, having some of Europe's most important colonies of seabirds, but there are superb beaches too, a remarkable tradition of fiddle music, the fire festival of Up Helly Aa, and some of the finest clifftop coastal walks you'll find anywhere.

SHETLAND

Opposite Mainland, puffin at Sumburgh Head **Overleaf** Unst, Sandwick Beach

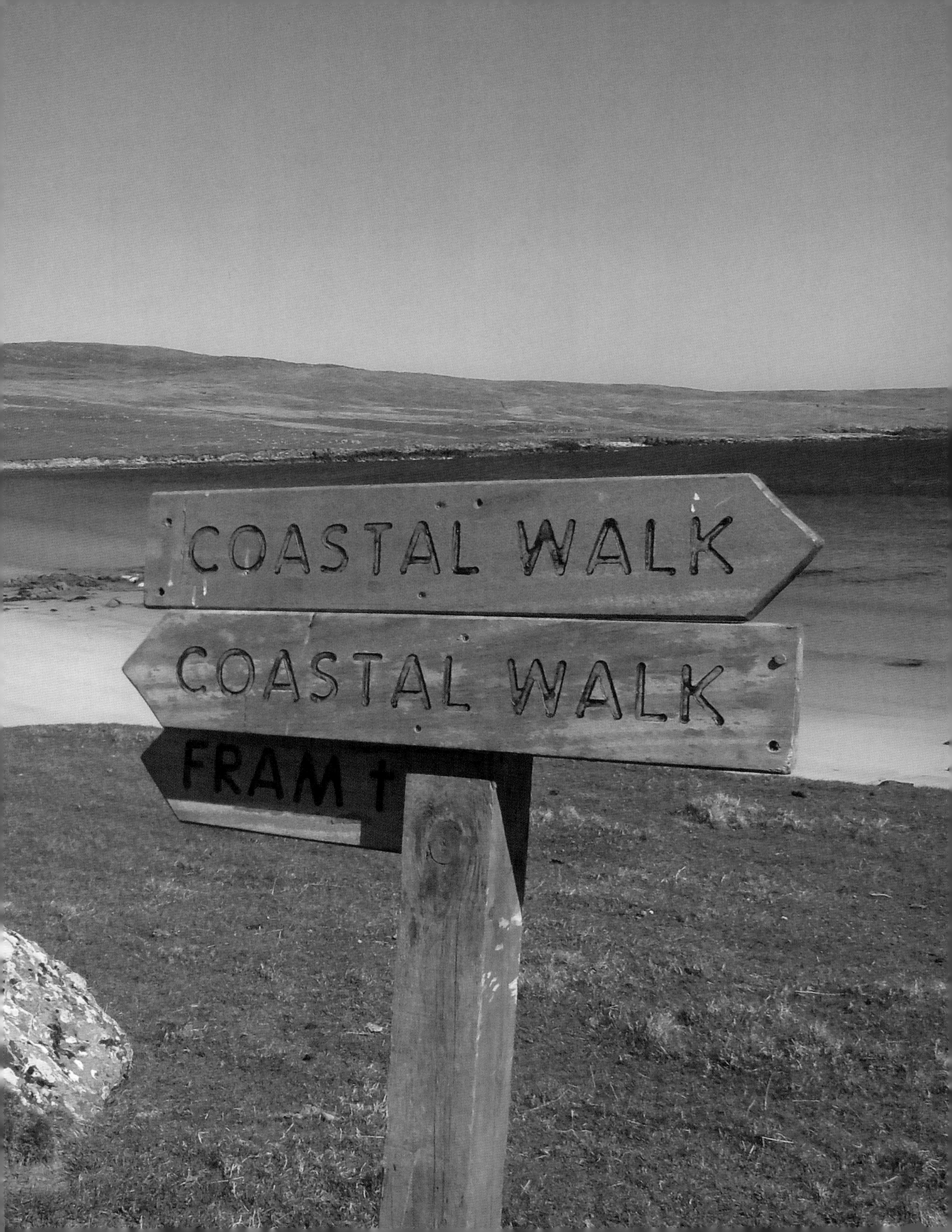
COASTAL WALK
COASTAL WALK
FRAM

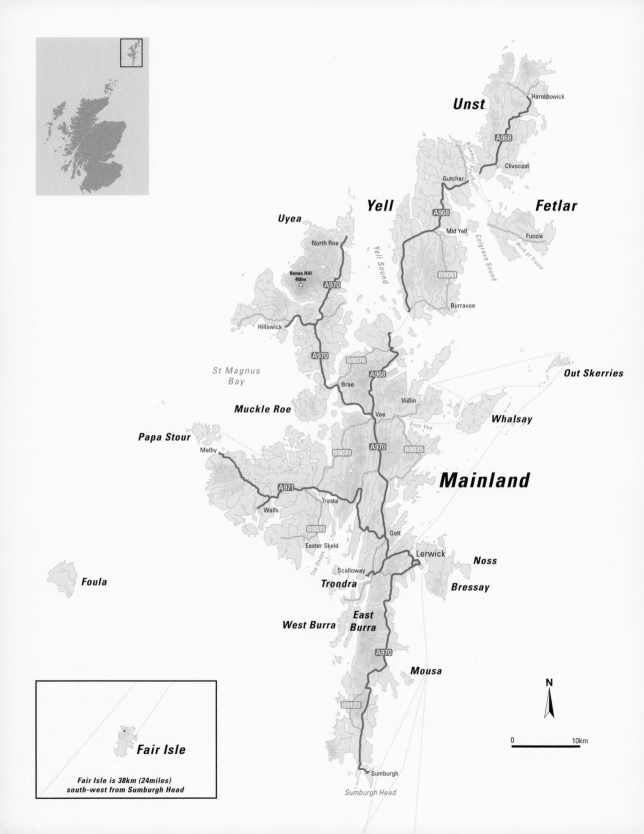

Mainland

With its capital Lerwick lying over 450 kilometres north of Edinburgh – and being considerably closer to Norway – Shetland truly feels a place apart from the rest of Scotland. Its largest island, Mainland, is long and straggly with innumerable long inlets – known as Voes – and countless headlands and peninsulas. While the massive oil terminal at Sullom Voe has brought wealth to this remote outpost, the coastal scenery, improbably rich with natural arches, stacks and caves, is simply magnificent.

The large vehicle ferries travel overnight – sea conditions permitting – between Aberdeen and Lerwick, taking twelve to fourteen hours depending on whether the boat is calling at Orkney along the way. The alternative is to take a flight to Sumburgh Airport towards the southern end of Mainland; there are connections to Aberdeen, Inverness, Orkney, Glasgow, Edinburgh, Manchester and Bergen. There's a good range of shops, services, places to eat and accommodation available, heavily concentrated in Lerwick.

Catch some jigs and reels

Shetland has a vibrant community music scene and is especially renowned for its fiddle music. Scotland's most famous fiddler, Aly Bain, is from Shetland, as are more recent bands such as Fiddlers' Bid. There's a wide-ranging programme of concerts held at Lerwick's Mareel arts centre, but perhaps the best way to experience some fine fiddling is in one of the pubs around the town. Try the Lounge Bar on Mounthooly Street – or ask a local.

Discover the Dark Side at Scalloway Castle

While Lerwick is the heart of Shetland today, the original capital was at nearby Scalloway, clustered around its impressive ruined castle.

This was built by Patrick Stewart – nicknamed 'Black Patie' due to his oppressive rule over the islands. He is said to have used forced labour to build this forbidding keep in 1599, but eventually his wicked ways caught up with him and he was forced to flee Shetland in 1609, before being executed in Edinburgh. The castle is free and usually unlocked – if not then the key can be obtained from the Scalloway Museum adjacent.

Cross the tombolo to St Ninian's Isle

Magnificent sandy beaches aren't perhaps the first thing you'd imagine finding on Shetland, but this wonderful stretch of perfect shell sand must rank amongst the finest in the country. The beach here is a tombolo, a narrow strip of sand that forms a link from Mainland to St Ninian's Isle. It's only covered at exceptional tides, so whether wandering across it to St Ninian's counts as another island bagged is up to you! Once across it's well worth walking around the coastline of the isle to take in the magnificent scenery. The ruins of the ancient chapel here yielded one of Shetland's richest archaeological finds, the St Ninian's hoard, replicas of which can be seen at the museum in Lerwick.

Get up close with a puffin at Sumburgh Head

The lighthouse complex at the southernmost tip of Mainland is one of Shetland's most popular attractions. There are displays on marine life, you can visit the engine room that powered the foghorns, have a cuppa in the cafe, and climb the wee tower for a stunning outlook over the open ocean towards the Fair Isle. What draws most visitors to make the trip though is a chance to view the bird colonies – and most especially the puffins. There are many viewing points around the headland, giving a chance to get close to these most magical of seabirds.

Uncover the many layers of the past at Jarlshof

A short distance north from Sumburgh Head is Jarlshof, one of the most fascinating archaeological sites in the whole of the UK. A community was first established here around 2700 BC and people lived on the site continuously for the next 4,000 years, leaving an entire smorgasbord of ancient remains for archaeologists and modern visitors to drool over. Walk around the well-preserved remains of oval Bronze Age houses, an Iron Age broch and wheelhouse, and Norse longhouses which may have been built cheek by jowl with the medieval farmstead on the site. The most recent building is a laird's house dating from the sixteenth century. Jarlshof is open between April and September and there is an entrance charge.

Sample the very best fish and chips at Frankie's

The tiny village of Brae in the north of Mainland is the unlikely setting for one of Britain's finest fish and chip shops. Frankie's has not only been a winner of the award for the best in the UK, it operates with a real eye for sustainability. Its owner even scooped a British Empire Medal in the Queen's Birthday Honours list for her services to fish and chips. The place has a small sit-in area as well as operating as a takeaway; if you can manage to resist perfect fish and home-made chips then they do crab claws, langoustines, scallops, local mussels … yes, you'll need to come back more than once.
www.frankiesfishandchips.com

Get wind-blasted at Esha Ness

The westernmost tip of the Northmavine peninsula well repays the long drive to get there. A squat lighthouse stands atop the incredibly convoluted coastline, and a short walk northwards along the clifftops revealing an intricate array of deep geos, blocky stacks and natural arches. It's bleak, bare and completely exposed to the prevailing westerly winds – an unforgiving place to be when the winter storms hit, but quite unforgettable. Keen walkers can take a much longer fourteen-kilometre circular hike right around the headland, using minor roads to cross the hinterland from Bordigarth to Tangwick.

Visit the haunting ruins of Fethaland

The 'Isle of Fethaland' may not really be an island in itself, but this shouldn't deter keen island baggers from making time to experience this far-flung corner of Shetland Mainland. Northmavine's road terminates just short of Isbister, and from here you have to hike almost four kilometres of rough track to reach the atmospheric ruins. The site was inhabited from prehistoric times, but most of the ruins you see today are of a salmon fishing station that operated from the 1600s until the early twentieth century. Workers manned up to sixty open rowboats known as sixareens, which incredibly used to fish from here to the edge of the continental shelf – eighty kilometres out to the west. Beyond the ruins is the northernmost part of Mainland, where a small lighthouse offers superb views along the coast to Uyea, out to the Ramna Stacks and across to Yell.

Climb Ronas Hill

At 450 metres, Shetland's highest hill is not a place of dizzying summitry, instead being the utmost dome of the vast, utterly empty and windswept North Roe plateau. The ascent is eased by a tarmac road that climbs steeply up to the telecoms equipment on nearby Collafirth Hill,

---

1 **Mainland**, Jarlshof 2 **Mainland**, fiddle music in the Lounge Bar, Lerwick 3 **Mainland**, ruins at Fethaland
4 **Mainland**, St Ninian's beach and isle 5 **Mainland**, Frankie's Fish and Chips **Photo:** Frankie's 6 **Mainland**, Esha Ness

but the hike from here – even though it only involves another 270 metres or so of ascent – should not be underestimated. The bare, stony tundra can make navigation a serious challenge when the frequent mists come down, but on a good day the view from the highest cairn is superb, taking in all Northmavine and far beyond.

Visit the great stacks of Silwick and Westerwick

The wild and deeply indented coastline of West Mainland is packed with interest, but it is the little-known section south of Silwick and Westerwick that is perhaps the most dramatic of all. You can walk the rugged coastline between these two farmsteads and beyond to the west – there's no path but every step reveals remarkable rock features. The many spires of castellated Erne's Stack are followed by the fine individual tower of the Skerry of the Wick, surrounded by grand cliffs. Beyond Westerwick is the rock architecture of the Giltarump, and if you are full of energy you can continue around the coast all the way to the remains of the Culswick broch.

Attend an Up Helly Aa

This Viking-themed fire festival dates back to the nineteenth century, but it has grown to become the best known of all the events on Scotland's islands. There are actually many Up Helly Aas held all around Shetland through January, but the one in Lerwick on the last Tuesday of the month is by far the largest.

There are forty-six squads totalling 1,000 men – women only take part in the Up Helly Aas outside of Lerwick – and one man each year is chosen as the Guizer Jarl, a great honour, and his squad becomes the Jarl's squad for that year. A great amount of care goes into the construction of the outfits every year, as well as the boat which is burnt at the end of a great torchlit procession for all the squads.

Less well known outside Shetland are the events in the halls that follow, as every hall around Lerwick puts on a ceilidh. Every squad of men then tours around the town throughout all the hours of the night, and every man must dance with a woman in every hall. Only the Jarl's squad are Vikings – all the other squads choose their own humorous outfits and perform a comic routine at each hall, often poking fun at local characters and politics. It's first and foremost a huge community event, but if you are lucky enough to be in Lerwick on Up Helly Aa, ask at the tourist office or check the local paper to see if any of the halls have spare tickets for visitors – it's an experience you'll never forget.

Bressay

The fifth largest island in Shetland, Bressay lies just offshore from Lerwick and shelters the harbour from easterly winds. Most of the population of around 350 people lives on the western side of the island, many of them commuting to work on Mainland. The interior rises to wild moorlands before descending to the more exposed and isolated east coast.

The island is served by regular vehicle ferries from the centre of Lerwick, taking around ten minutes to cross Bressay Sound. Bressay has a single hotel and a community shop.

Climb the Ward

The highest hill on Bressay, the Ward, topped by television and radio transmitter masts, is a prominent landmark from Lerwick, so it comes as little surprise that it's a really superb viewpoint. An excellent track leads

1 Mainland, Westerwick 2 Mainland, Scalloway Castle 3 Mainland, Ronas Hill 4 and 5 Mainland, Up Helly Aa, Lerwick

up to the 226-metre summit from the housing development at Glebe, making for a straightforward walk or even a mountain bike ride if you are fit enough. If you decide to extend the walk and leave the track, the going is tough over peat-hagged moorland and the area can be full of aggressive bonxies (great skuas) during the breeding season.

See the arch under Kirkabister Ness

The lighthouse complex at Kirkabister Ness provides a guide for ships heading north into the Bressay Sound. As you approach the lighthouse along the road from Kirkabister the whitewashed buildings look picturesque enough, but the true drama of the location is only revealed to those prepared to do a little more exploring. Head along the coast to the east of the lighthouse and you'll see that it's built almost on top of a fine natural rock arch. The light is still active but

automated, and the former keepers' cottages are available for holiday rentals.

Noss

The island of Noss is rather hidden away behind its larger neighbour Bressay, but don't let this shyness deter you from visiting – it's an unmissable gem for island baggers. Fringed by some spectacular cliffs, Noss is one of the most important sites for breeding seabirds in Scotland and is a National Nature Reserve. Its name comes from the Norse word for nose, and likely refers to the great promontory of Noss Head.

To reach Noss, first access the parking area on the far side of Bressay just before the track descends to Noss Sound. From here, a small inflatable boat ferries visitors across the narrows during the summer season, weather permitting – the crossing is often an adventure in itself.

The sound is a hotspot for sightings of orca, so keep your eyes peeled. Once on the island the only facility is the visitor centre, which has toilets.

Blow your mind at Noss Head

The eight-kilometre circular walk around Noss's coastline takes around four hours and is one of the finest in all Shetland. The island's interior hosts the world's fourth largest colony of bonxies (great skuas); there are otters to be seen along the west coast; eiders, shags and black guillemots (tysties) abound; and plenty of puffins top the southern cliffs. The highlight, however, is undoubtedly the climb up to the top of the 180-metre vertical cliffs of Noss Head – or the Noup of Noss. The cliffs are home to 25,000 guillemots and 10,000 pairs of beautiful gannets. Watching the latter dive for fish from above is enough to fill the coolest head with vertigo.

Mousa

Just off the east coast of Mainland, Mousa is another island nature reserve, this time in the ownership of the RSPB. It provides a home for colonies of grey and common seals, black guillemots (tysties) and storm petrels. Although today Mousa is uninhabited, human occupation can be traced back over 3,000 years – most spectacularly in the island's celebrated Iron Age broch.

A private passenger boat operates trips out to the island from Sandsayre pier on Mainland throughout the summer months and booking is recommended. There are public toilets and a small museum in Sandsayre, but no facilities on Mousa itself.

Stand atop the greatest of brochs

Reached by a fifteen-minute walk southwards from the jetty is a truly magnificent structure, the Mousa broch. Defensive structures built during the Iron Age, brochs occur on many islands and along Scotland's north and west coastlines, but Mousa is by far the best preserved of them all. Built around 300 BC with the most remarkable craftsmanship, this circular drystone tower still stands to a height of thirteen metres. The broch has two parallel walls, and between them are various smaller chambers, and a stone staircase that still allows visitors to ascend to the top. There are great views across the Mousa Sound – watch out for orca passing through – and you may note the more ruinous remains of the Broch of Burraland on the opposite side of the channel.

Witness the return of the storm petrels

For night-time visitors to Mousa broch, an even more special experience awaits. From late May until mid-July, hundreds of storm petrels return to their nests on the broch walls, drystane dykes and the beach. Special boat trips operate several times a week to take visitors out to witness this great spectacle. As darkness falls, the ancient, lichen-encrusted walls of the broch echo with the strange, eerie, troll-like calls of these tiny but remarkable seabirds that spend all the rest of their lives out at sea.

Trondra

The Scalloway Islands lie south of the town and provide shelter to its harbour. They were steadily losing their population until 1971, when new road bridges were built linking Trondra to Mainland, and then onwards from Trondra to West and East Burra. Since then the population has recovered and now stands at over a hundred. For most visitors, Trondra is a stepping stone en route to its neighbours.

Experience a slice of Shetland croft life

Of the visitors who do pause on Trondra, most are headed for the Burland Croft Trail. The Isbister family have worked the croft here since the 1970s, maintaining local Shetland breeds of animals and poultry as well as raising crops. In the summer months they welcome visitors and it's a great chance especially for children to meet and feed the animals which include Shetland ponies, cows, sheep, pigs and ducks.

West Burra

Over nine kilometres in length but never much more than a kilometre wide, West Burra is home to over 700 people, with the largest settlement at Hamnavoe in the north. Here is the Scalloway Islands' only shop and petrol station, and bed and breakfast is also available. There is also low-cost accommodation at the Bridge End Outdoor Centre near the bridge to East Burra.

West Burra is connected to mainland Shetland by road bridges via the neighbouring island of Trondra.

Visit Meal beach

Just outside Hamnavoe is a parking area from where a boardwalk path leads down to this beautiful sandy beach. Meal faces south, sheltered from the prevailing winds, and is a popular beach by Shetland standards – which means you *might* even find someone else here at the same time. If the temperature isn't high enough for sunbathing, you can walk west along the coast to visit the rocky Fugla Ness peninsula and on into Hamnavoe.

Cross Banna Min

At the southern end of West Burra's road is the restored East House – sometimes open as a museum – and a parking area. A short stroll from here leads to one of Shetland's finest and lesser known beaches, Banna Min. The sandy bay here is on the north side of the narrow tombolo that connects the wild Kettla Ness peninsula to the rest of the island. The beach is well sheltered from most directions, and if you tire of relaxing then there's the fine cliffs of Kettla Ness to explore. Head over the Ward to reach the impressive rock scenery around the Heugg.

East Burra

If you've followed the road from Mainland over the bridges to Trondra and then West Burra, a much smaller bridge makes the onward connection to East Burra, which is the end of the line. East Burra has a much smaller population than its neighbour, and feels rather sandwiched between it and the forbidding and bare Clift Hills on the nearest part of Mainland.

Ascend the Ward of Symbister

The road south ends at Houss and the island narrows just beyond here at Ayre Dyke, though there is no spectacular beach like that at Banna Min on West Burra. A track leads across to the Houss Ness peninsula, whose open coastline provides a great place to explore. Be sure to climb to the top of the Ward of Symbister for comprehensive views over this island group and its long voes and sounds.

Papa Stour

Boasting a fantastical coastline with some of Britain's finest sea caves, arches, tunnels and stacks, a visit to Papa Stour is a wonderful experience. Often known locally simply as Papa,

the island has a population of fewer than twenty, all in the Biggings area in the east, while the western part is magnificently wild and exposed.

Papa Stour is connected to Mainland by a ferry from West Burrafirth which takes forty minutes and operates four days a week, though only three of these allow time for a day trip. All sailings must be pre-booked. The ferryboat, the *Snolda*, does take vehicles, but there is little point in visitors bringing cars to the island as there is only two kilometres of road. There is also an airstrip on the island, with a very limited flight schedule from Tingwall airport near Lerwick. The toilets and small waiting room above the pier are the main facilities for visitors, though it may be possible to rent a self-catering cottage.

Visit the kirk and beach

Papa's narrow strip of tarmac leads past a partly reconstructed stofa – a medieval Norse house – en route to the church. The current kirk dates back to 1806, replacing an earlier thatched one that had partly collapsed some years before. It's well worth heading inside to see the beautiful stained-glass window by Victor Noble Rainbird – it commemorates the six men from Papa who lost their lives in the First World War. A short stroll across croftland leads to Kirk Sand, probably the finest beach on the island.

Cross the arch at Aesha Head

Papa Stour's most magnificent coastal scenery is reserved for those who undertake a long and rough hike to visit its western cliffs. Here there's a vast array of remarkable cliff features, including Kirstan's Hole – a great blowhole – and a range of stacks and geos. Offshore are the dramatic islets of Fogla Skerry and Lyra Skerry – both pierced by tunnels – and the UK's longest subterranean sea passage under Virda Field, though the latter can only be seen from the sea. It's hard to pick out a single highlight, but a walk over the spectacular arch that cuts through Aesha Head is difficult to surpass.

Muckle Roe

This almost circular island is five kilometres across and linked to Shetland Mainland by the Muckle Roe bridge over the Roe Sound. Much of the island is composed of red granite, giving rise to its name – based on old Norse and Scots – which means 'big red island'. The population of around 130 lives along the eastern coastal strip, while the centre rises to rugged hills, falling in fine cliffs to the south and west.

Hike to the light

Muckle Roe has the reputation of having some of Shetland's finest walking, and the two-kilometre-long path to its tiny lighthouse gives a dramatic and memorable outing. Beginning from Little-ayre, a track soon leads to the fine bay of Muckle Ayre. A rugged path then climbs steeply, crossing a boggy area, before embarking on a fine traverse high above the coast. After reaching Gilsa Water it climbs again briefly before descending past the great collapsed cave known as the Hole of Hellier. The modern lighthouse is a short distance beyond, in as wild and dramatic a spot as you could hope for. Watch out for seals around the bases of the Murbie Stacks.

Visit the Hams

It is possible to extend the above walk by a very rugged but dramatic route along the clifftops from the light to the bays of the South and North Hams, or you can reach them much more easily by following a Land Rover track for four kilometres each way direct from Little-ayre. South Ham was once used for smuggling from the Faroes; the ruins at Burg overlook this open and beautiful bay. The North Ham is much narrower and more dramatic with spectacular cliffs as well as the remains of an old Norse mill.

Uyea

This small tidal island off the north-western extremity of Mainland's Northmavine has built a reputation for its remoteness and the beauty of its setting. Reaching Uyea on foot is a real challenge.

An Uyea adventure

Just getting to see Uyea from Sandvoe is a tough, strenuous and wild walk in itself – either following the pathless clifftops or the track inland, the circuit of both routes making for a full day's fifteen-and-a-half-kilometre adventure as rugged as any hillwalk. The island is separated from Mainland by a stretch of beautiful tidal sand and reaching this point will be more than enough for most. Actually crossing to Uyea requires timing the walk perfectly with the tides, combined with a hazardous and slippery rock descent to reach the beach. There's a very real chance of becoming stranded.

Yell

For many visitors Yell is merely a large stepping stone en route during their pilgrimage to the most northerly inhabited island, Unst. However, if you turn aside from the rather bleak journey along the main road there is plenty to explore here. It's the second largest of all the Shetland Isles after Mainland, with a population just short of a thousand.

The southern end of the island at Ulsta is linked to Toft on Mainland by a regular vehicle ferry service, while Gutcher at the north end has onward ferries to the islands of Unst and Fetlar. Yell has general stores – and petrol stations – at Mid Yell and Aywick; Mid Yell also has a leisure

centre and swimming pool. Accommodation is available in bed and breakfasts or in the Windhouse Lodge camping 'böds' – a form of very basic hostel unique to Shetland.

See the White Wife of Otterswick

This striking white structure was originally the figurehead of the German ship *Bohus* that sank nearby in 1924 during a storm. Four of the thirty-nine crew were drowned, including Cadet Eberth who saved four of his shipmates before losing his own life. The figurehead you see now was washed ashore later that year and was erected by locals within sight of the sinking. It has been restored and was unveiled as an official monument in 1989.

Watch an otter

Shetland is one of the best places in the world to watch European otters, and out of all the Shetland Isles, Yell is pre-eminent for otter lovers. They can be seen all around the coast, particularly on the eastern side, with regular sightings from Burra Ness to Burravoe, with – as you might expect – Otterswick in between being a particular hotspot. Otters have very keen senses so you'll need to be very quiet, avoid standing out on the skyline and approach from downwind, otherwise they'll be gone long before you could spot them. If you get lucky, watching them fishing and coming ashore to eat is an experience you'll never forget.

The Gloup memorial

This moving memorial commemorates Shetland's greatest fishing tragedy, and takes the form of a fisherwife looking out to sea with her child, scanning the horizon for those who were never coming back. It was built in 1981, a hundred years after the day

when fifty-eight fishermen on ten boats were lost in an unexpected storm. These men left behind thirty-four widows and eighty-five now-fatherless children. Most of the boats were open sixareens which were traditional in Shetland. Sixareens rowed far into open sea from a base fishing station or haaf, to fish for two or three days at a time. The disaster decimated the local community and began the decline of the use of sixareens. The memorial is a short stroll from the road end and overlooks the remarkable long, deep channel of Gloup Voe.

Sunbathe on the Sands of Breckon

Yell isn't commonly associated with fine sandy beaches, but actually it has a couple of real gems. West Sandwick has a fine beach looking out to an islet, but it is the Sands of Breckon in the north that is really quite unmissable. There's parking at Breckon from which the beach is just a short, signposted stroll. The graceful arc of sand is sheltered by the long, narrow peninsula of the Ness of Houlland. If you are looking for a hike then you can follow the rough coastline to the west, heading around Gloup Ness to reach Gloup and its memorial.

Burra Voe

The long inlet of Burra Voe is on the southern coastline, sheltered by the low-lying peninsula of Heoga Ness. A circuit around the latter makes for a fine five-kilometre walk, which can be extended to Ladies Hole for a chance to spot a puffin and other seabirds. Make sure you also explore the Old Haa, a beautiful seventeenth-century house that acts as Yell's museum – and tearoom.

Unst

The most northerly inhabited island in Britain, Unst is the final outpost before the vast sea stretches away towards the Arctic. The spectacular seabird colonies of Hermaness have brought it fame, but there's actually a wide array of scenery to discover here, along with superb beaches and a distinctive heritage.

Unst is served by regular car ferries linking the pier at Belmont with Gutcher on neighbouring Yell (the same boat also provides a connection to Fetlar). There's a leisure centre with swimming pool at Baltasound, a couple of shops and several accommodation options including a hotel, bed and breakfast and a range of self-catering rentals.

See Muckle Flugga from Hermaness

The cliffs of Hermaness – the most northerly part of Unst – are a spectacular National Nature Reserve and one of Shetland's most essential places to experience. It's hard to know where to begin when describing them: there are 50,000 pairs of puffins, one of the most aggressive colonies of bonxies in all the isles, a stunning gannetry at the Neap with vast vertical walls of rock, and the view looks out to the lighthouse on Muckle Flugga – the most northerly landfall in the UK.

There's a visitor centre in the lighthouse shore station just below the car park. To reach the cliffs, a well-marked walkway leads north and then west across bleak moorland where the bonxies are much in evidence in season. Little can prepare you for suddenly reaching the rim of the cliffs and their great plunge to the endless ocean. The puffins are all around from here – a right turn along the cliffs leads to increasingly rough terrain and a closer view of Muckle Flugga, whereas a left turn heads for the gannetry. Either way, it's not a place you'll forget.

Find Edmonston's chickweed at the Keen of Hamar

Away from the drama of Hermaness, Unst actually has a second National Nature Reserve. There is a car park at Littlehamar and then signs indicate the route to the reserve, where the landscape is so bare it appears almost lunar. This is caused by the serpentine rocks here, which were formed in the sea before being thrown up by a massive earth movement around 400 million years ago. Serpentinite is rarely found on the surface; it has weathered to a thin soil, but this bare place resembles how much of Northern Europe would have appeared after glaciers retreated at the end of the last Ice Age.

A close inspection reveals that an array of rare vegetation actually grows here. The most celebrated is the white flowers of Edmonston's chickweed, which is also known as 'Shetland mouse-ear' – a plant that grows only on serpentine on Unst. A twelve-year-old local boy named Thomas Edmondston discovered it; he went on to become a professor of botany and wrote a book on Shetland's flora before being tragically killed on a scientific expedition to South America at the age of twenty.

Take a break at Bobby's bus shelter

At a bend in the A968 road between Baltasound and Haroldswick stands a humble bus shelter that has become famed around the world. On wind-blasted Unst you really need a shelter when waiting for a bus, so when the council removed it in 1996, local boy Bobby Macaulay wrote to the local paper to complain and ask for a new one.

Following a petition the new shelter was delivered, and soon afterwards items and

1 **Unst**, gannetry at the Neap, Herma Ness   2 **Unst**, bonxie – or great skua   3 **Unst**, view to Muckle Flugga
4 **Unst**, Muness castle   5 **Unst**, Bobby's bus shelter   6 **Unst**, Edmonston's chickweed   7 **Unst**, Sandwick beach

furniture began to mysteriously appear in it. Soon there was a sofa, carpet and curtains, and a cult was born. The shelter is now redecorated every few years by local volunteers and has featured a variety of themes. It has even hosted a two-seater film festival screening, attended by Mark Kermode and his mum. If you want to get really off the wall, you could even just sit in it and wait for a bus.

Discover the Viking past at Sandwick Beach

There's a fine beach at Norwick beyond the old RAF base at Saxa Vord, but the best on Unst is undoubtedly Sandwick on a lonely stretch of the east coast. This half-kilometre stretch of sand is a magical place to relax on a fine summer's day, but if the weather is wild it's also a great area to explore.

The area around the beach has some important archaeological sites. There are the remains of a Norse longhouse, now becoming engulfed by the sands, two Pictish burial sites, and a cemetery containing the ruins of a Viking chapel – connected with the farmstead of Framgord. The cemetery is still in use – coffins are now brought in by tractor, but the mourners have to make the walk themselves. It's possible to explore the coastline further north to visit the deserted township of Colvadale.

Explore Muness Castle

Britain's most northerly medieval castle is found three kilometres east of Uyeasound. Its grey stone walls still stand strong against the worst storms that batter Unst, with two and a half of its original three storeys relatively intact. The castle is free to enter – it's either unlocked, or there's a sign letting you know where you can collect the key – and once inside you can explore the kitchens and cellars downstairs and the now open great hall above.

Fetlar

Despite being the fourth largest of the Shetland isles, Fetlar is little visited, lying off the usual tourist route north up through Yell to Unst. It is home to around sixty people and is probably best known for its RSPB reserve, though there's a fine beach at the Sand of Tresta and some dramatic coastal cliffs.

The island is served by the Bluemull vehicle ferry that provides a link to both Unst and Yell, though only a few of the services each day call at Fetlar. There's a heritage centre at Houbie in the south of the island, a bed and breakfast and a self-catering property to rent – in addition to the basic hostel or böd at Aithbank. Note that there is no petrol station on Fetlar.

See the red-necked phalarope

Fetlar has long been something of a mecca for keen twitchers, with all kinds of unexpected birds turning up; famously it was home to a pair of breeding snowy owls in the 1960s and 1970s. Most birders, however, head here to see another species, the red-necked phalarope, as the island hosts more than half of the UK population. Unusually it's the female rather than the male that has the distinctive bright plumage, and it's the male that does the incubating and chick rearing. There's a hide at the Mires of Funzie, but the Loch of Funzie itself is where you are most likely to get a good look at this lovely wee bird.

Cross the arch at the Snap

The Snap is the name of the headland at the southern end of the Funzie Ness peninsula, the whole of which provides for an excellent wild coastal walk. Head south from the Haa of Funzie; the going is rugged, but the coastal scenery is superb. The highlight is a magnificent

1 Fetlar, Stranburgh Head   **2 Fetlar**, Aithbank böd   **3 Fetlar**, arch at the Snap

rock arch just before reaching the headland – you can walk out over it, but be careful near the unprotected cliff edge, especially when the winds are up.

Visit Strandburgh Ness

A narrow neck of land connects Inner Brough to the rest of Fetlar, with Viking ruins to pass through to reach the furthest point. This was once the site of the largest Norse monastic settlement in Shetland. Incredibly there are further remains on the Outer Brough beyond, which is separated by a cliff-girt channel of the wildest seas.

The shortest route to the headland is from the croft at Everland, heading past an old ruin and over stiles to reach the coast at the Wick of Gruting. From here you can continue past the remains of some Norse mills to reach Strandburgh Ness. It's possible to make a nine-and-a-half-kilometre circuit by following the east coast to the Haa of Funzie, but this stretch is wild and rough, with some coastal cliffs and arches.

Stay at Aithbank böd

In Shetland a böd was originally a building that temporarily housed fishermen during the fishing season. The word is now used to describe a basic type of hostel unique to Shetland – similar in concept to camping barns in England. Böds provide low-cost accommodation with few facilities – some have no electricity or even lighting, though all have at least cold water and toilet facilities. They can be booked through the Shetland Amenity Trust in Lerwick.

The böd at Aithbank is one of the finest, with a shower and cooking facilities. It was once the home to a legendary local storyteller – Jamsie Laurensen – and has superb views along the coastline.

www.camping-bods.com

Whalsay

Home to over a thousand people, Whalsay is a surprisingly well-populated and prosperous island. It's the heart of Shetland's fishing industry, and its fertile hinterland is well-crofted. In the 1930s and 1940s it was the home of Christopher Murray Grieve – better known as Hugh MacDiarmid, regarded as one of the greatest Scots poets. Active politically, he championed Scottish independence and was one of the founders of the National Party of Scotland, a forerunner of the current Scottish National Party.

Whalsay is served by car ferries from Laxo and Vidlin on the mainland, with the crossing taking around thirty minutes. The capital Symbister has a shop, and the house that Hugh MacDiarmid lived in is now a böd providing basic accommodation. The island also boasts the UK's most northerly eighteen-hole golf course.

Hear about the Hanseatic League

The picturesque stone-built pier house at Symbister is now a museum telling the story of a forgotten part of Shetland history. Ships from ports in northern Germany once visited Shetland every summer, bringing a variety of goods which they traded with Shetland fish. The museum building was owned by these German merchants, and today it tells the story of this trade between the island and what was known as the Hanseatic League. The union between Scotland and England in 1707 brought in its wake new import duties that forced a stop to this international trade.

Climb the Ward

The highest point on Whalsay is the Ward of Clett (119 metres), a fairly short and straightforward walk from the ferry pier. A track leads up to the summit – marked by a trig point and some old military buildings – which provides a superb outlook over the whole of the island as well as over to Out Skerries, Bressay and Noss.

1 Whalsay, view from the Ward **2 Out Skerries,** bridge linking Bruray and Housay **3 Whalsay,** pierhouse museum
4 Out Skerries, Grunay and the Skerries lighthouse from Bruray

Out Skerries

Simply known locally as Da Skerries, Out Skerries consists of three small islands – Bruray, Housay and Grunay – and numerously tiny islets and stacks, together forming the easternmost part of Scotland. Bruray and Housay are both inhabited and are linked by a bridge, whereas Grunay is now deserted.

Skerries is connected to Mainland Shetland by ferries from Vidlin (ninety minutes) and, less often, from Lerwick (two and a half hours). There are a few days each week when it is possible to make a day trip to the island, though the crossing is often affected by rough seas. There are also scheduled flights from the Tingwall airstrip near Lerwick. There is a tiny shop on both islands, and bed and breakfast accommodation is available.

See the Skerries light from Bruray
The lighthouse on the rocky islet of Bound Skerry is the tallest in Shetland, an elegant

tower rising to thirty metres. The lighthouse keepers lived on neighbouring Grunay and were bombed during the Second World War. Since the light was automated in 1972 Grunay has been uninhabited. Probably the best view of the lighthouse is off the ferry from Vidlin as it heads round the north side of Bruray, and it's a striking sight as it turns into the narrow Northeast Mouth to Skerries' fine natural harbour.

Ramble round Housay
It's possible to walk almost right around the coastline of both Bruray and Housay, crossing the Skerries Bridge that has linked them since 1957. There is no path and the going is rough in places on this twelve-kilometre route, and the south-westernmost extremity, the Ward of Mioness, is cut off from the rest of Housay by a natural chasm at the back of Trolli Geo. It's worth climbing to the top of Bruray Ward to the north of the airstrip; while only fifty-three metres high it gives fine views over the vast ocean – and to the eastern coast of Mainland Shetland if the weather is clear.

1 Fair Isle, cliffs below Ward Hill   **2** Fair Isle, Ward Hill summit   **3** Fair Isle, bonxie

Fair Isle

Lying some thirty-nine kilometres south-west from Sumburgh Head on Shetland Mainland, the Fair Isle is the UK's most isolated permanently inhabited island. Set almost midway between Shetland and Orkney, this remote outpost is home to around fifty people. Its name is well known for its woollen knitwear, and for featuring in the BBC Radio 4 shipping forecasts. Amongst keen twitchers it has almost legendary status as a watch point for migrating birds.

Getting to Fair Isle is an adventure in itself. There are scheduled flights on a tiny nine-seater plane from Tingwall outside Lerwick; the flight takes only thirty minutes and can allow for day trips. Three times a week the *Good Shepherd IV* passenger ferry sails between Fair Isle and Grutness Pier near Sumburgh Head – this takes two and a half hours. Both flights and ferry are frequently cancelled due to adverse weather, and if you do travel to Fair Isle be aware that you may not be able to leave the island on the day you expected! There is fully catered accommodation at the South Light and a couple of full-board guest houses. The bird observatory, first set up in old naval huts in 1948 and replaced by a new building in 2010, was sadly destroyed by fire in 2019.

Climb Ward Hill

A track leads from the north side of the aircraft landing strip to a series of communications masts, and from there a final steeper climb leads to the Fair Isle's highest summit – Ward Hill (217 metres). The area is littered with the scattered remains of an old RAF radar base, but nothing can distract from the unique views – a 360-degree sweep of open ocean.

The whole of the Fair Isle is in view, with Malcolm's Head and the Sheep Rock both prominent, while to the west the slope falls rapidly to reach the brim of the great cliffs of the island's west coast. A rougher return can be made by following these massive clifftops southwards, passing high above gannet colonies, around geos and past high stacks before reaching a massive stone wall that leads back towards the airstrip.

See the Sheep Rock

This massive rocky outcrop – topped with a small area of grass – is connected to Fair Isle's eastern coastline and stands out as the island's most distinctive landmark. Incredibly it was used – as its name suggests – for grazing sheep in summer until 1977. As it is quite inaccessible, the sheep were hauled up by rope from boats below, with an incredibly precarious and dangerous path up being used by the crofters.

The rock is in view from most of the island, but to appreciate it up close you can reach it by following the coastline from either the north or south. The northern approach passes some fine arches and plenty of puffins in the breeding season.

Become a fully fledged twitcher

Fair Isle has long been famed as a great place to spot migrating birds. The first bird observatory was set up here in a complex of old naval huts back in 1948. It was replaced by purpose-built premises in 1969, and again in 2010 by a larger building that offered guest accommodation open to all and a place for birdwatching enthusiasts to meet up and exchange news of sightings. Sadly that building was totally destroyed by fire in 2019, although luckily the birding species logs and other scientific records had been digitised and were saved.

The work of the observatory, which is run by a charity, will continue and there are plans to rebuild and offer accommodation again as soon as possible. While staying at the observatory is a very special experience, with the opportunity to accompany the wardens on their early morning walks around the bird traps and contribute to the scientific work, exploring the island under your own steam is also very rewarding. Spend a day or more on the island, binoculars and bird book in hand, and you'll be surprised at how quickly you get drawn into the magical world of birding.

Get knitted

Fair Isle knitting patterns are known throughout the world, but it is only on the Fair Isle itself that the genuine, authentic product – marked by its trademark star motif – is produced by a handful of skilled local knitters. The sweaters rose to great popularity when the Prince of Wales (later to be crowned Edward VIII) wore one in 1921. A full hand-knit jumper is a major investment, but you can also get scarves and hats if you are looking for something more affordable.

Many of the knitters can be visited when you are on the island so that you can purchase their work direct. Enthusiasts should visit Shetland during Wool Week in the autumn when there is an extensive programme of events, exhibitions and open studio days throughout Shetland.

Foula

The spectacular – and spectacularly isolated – island of Foula lies over twenty kilometres west of Shetland Mainland. A tiny community lives along its eastern half in the straggly settlement of Hametoun, while to the west the land rises to sculpted hills, culminating in great cliffs that are the highest in all Shetland.

Reaching Foula is even more chancy than getting to Fair Isle. Again, there are scheduled flights on a tiny nine-seater plane from Tingwall outside Lerwick; these take only fifteen minutes and on certain days each week can allow a day trip. The plane gives amazing views over West Mainland before crossing the sea to Foula. There's also a passenger ferry twice a week from Walls, taking two and a quarter hours and carrying up to twelve people. Both the flights and ferry are frequently cancelled due to adverse weather – check on the day, and be aware that there's always a chance you'll be stranded on the island. There is no shop on Foula, and only very limited accommodation that must be arranged in advance.

Discover Da Sneck o da Smaalie

Da Sneck is a spectacular crack formed by a landslip that splits the great western cliffs of Foula. It is an excellent objective for a walk from the airstrip, heading up the wide, flat-bottomed glen of Da Daal that passes between Foula's big hills. The dramatic coastal cliffs are reached suddenly, with Da Sneck forming a long chasm. Do not attempt to descend into it, but you can walk along the grassy top of Da Sneck on either side. Look out for puffins that nest in burrows above the cliff edge nearby. To the south of Da Sneck the land rises to the great craggy summit of Da Noup – a great extension to the walk if you have the time and energy to make the outing into a hillwalk.

Survive da bonxies on Da Sneug

At 418 metres, Da Sneug is the highest summit on Foula, the culmination of an elegantly sculpted ridge that dominates much of the island. The ridge provides a direct route to the summit from the Baxter Chapel – which houses a mass of information on the island – near the airfield. Conditions underfoot are generally good, but there are few places in Britain as exposed to the elements as this. Another hazard are the bonxies or great skuas which attack walkers during nesting season – at such times it's best to carry a stick to hold above your head to fend them off.

Just before the summit are a group of prehistoric stones known as the Brethren, and the ground then rises to the final trig point and cairn and an unforgettable vista – a three-hour round trip from the airstrip. If you have the time the ridge continues from here, descending to 316 metres before a final rise to Da Kame – from where the land falls vertically for 370 metres to the sea. This is the highest sea cliff in Britain outside St Kilda, and is perhaps even more frightening. While it's possible to continue north-east above the coast, there's a very steep descent to make, and the easiest option is instead to retrace your steps.

The Islands: at a glance

Index

In the bag ...

The Firth of Forth
- [ ] Isle of May
- [ ] Bass Rock
- [ ] Craigleith
- [ ] Fidra
- [ ] Inchkeith
- [ ] Inchcolm
- [ ] Cramond Island

The Firth of Clyde
- [ ] Arran
- [ ] Pladda
- [ ] Holy Isle
- [ ] Bute
- [ ] Inchmarnock
- [ ] Great Cumbrae
- [ ] Little Cumbrae
- [ ] Ailsa Craig
- [ ] Davaar Island
- [ ] Sanda

Islay, Jura & Colonsay
- [ ] Islay
- [ ] Jura
- [ ] Colonsay
- [ ] Oronsay
- [ ] Gigha
- [ ] Cara

The Firth of Lorn & Loch Linnhe
- [ ] Seil
- [ ] Easdale
- [ ] Luing
- [ ] Shuna
- [ ] Lunga
- [ ] Scarba
- [ ] The Garvellachs
- [ ] Kerrera
- [ ] Lismore
- [ ] Eriska
- [ ] Island of Shuna

The Isle of Mull Group
- [ ] Mull
- [ ] Iona
- [ ] Erraid
- [ ] Ulva
- [ ] Gometra
- [ ] Inch Kenneth
- [ ] Little Colonsay
- [ ] Staffa
- [ ] Lunga and the Treshnish Islands
- [ ] Eorsa
- [ ] Carna
- [ ] Oronsay

Coll, Tiree & the Small Isles
- [ ] Tiree
- [ ] Coll
- [ ] Eigg
- [ ] Rum
- [ ] Canna
- [ ] Sanday
- [ ] Muck
- [ ] Eilean Shona

Skye & the North-West
- [ ] Skye
- [ ] Loch Bracadale Islands
- [ ] Soay
- [ ] Eilean Ban
- [ ] Pabay
- [ ] Scalpay
- [ ] Raasay
- [ ] Eilean Fladday
- [ ] Rona
- [ ] Isle of Ewe
- [ ] Gruinard Island
- [ ] Summer Isles
- [ ] Isle Martin
- [ ] Handa
- [ ] Rabbit Islands
- [ ] Eilean nan Ròn

The Outer Hebrides

- [ ] Lewis
- [ ] Eilean Chaluim Cille
- [ ] Great Bernera
- [ ] Pabbay (Loch Roag)
- [ ] Harris
- [ ] Scalpay
- [ ] Taransay
- [ ] Scarp
- [ ] Pabbay
- [ ] Flannan Isles
- [ ] St Kilda Archipelago
- [ ] Rockall
- [ ] North Rona
- [ ] Sula Sgeir
- [ ] Shiant Islands
- [ ] Berneray
- [ ] North Uist
- [ ] Vallay (Bhàlaigh)
- [ ] Baleshare (Baile Sear)
- [ ] Monach Isles
- [ ] Grimsay
- [ ] Ronay (Rònaigh)
- [ ] Benbecula (Beinn na Faoghla)
- [ ] Flodaigh (Fladda)
- [ ] South Uist
- [ ] Eriskay
- [ ] Barra
- [ ] Vatersay
- [ ] Fuday
- [ ] Bishop's Isles (Barra)

Orkney

- [ ] Mainland
- [ ] Brough of Birsay
- [ ] Lamb Holm
- [ ] Burray
- [ ] Hunda
- [ ] South Ronaldsay
- [ ] Hoy
- [ ] South Walls
- [ ] Graemsay

- [ ] Flotta
- [ ] Rousay
- [ ] Egilsay
- [ ] Wyre
- [ ] Westray
- [ ] Papa Westray
- [ ] Holm of Papa
- [ ] Shapinsay
- [ ] Eday
- [ ] Stronsay
- [ ] Papa Stronsay
- [ ] Sanday
- [ ] North Ronaldsay
- [ ] Copinsay
- [ ] Stroma
- [ ] Swona

Shetland

- [ ] Mainland
- [ ] Bressay
- [ ] Noss
- [ ] Mousa
- [ ] Trondra
- [ ] West Burra
- [ ] East Burra
- [ ] Papa Stour
- [ ] Muckle Roe
- [ ] Uyea
- [ ] Yell
- [ ] Unst
- [ ] Fetlar
- [ ] Whalsay
- [ ] Out Skerries
- [ ] Fair Isle
- [ ] Foula

Overleaf Lewis, cleared village of Stiomrabhaigh

243